Grief: journey to GOD and us

Grief: journey to GOD and us

A Sequel to

Quiet Love … eyes to see and words to tell the truths that are most true

Eric C. Bow

ISBN 978-1-7750338-0-6

Published by Patricia Bow Inc

www.execulink.com/~thebows/patricia.htm

Distributed by Lulu Press

www.lulu.com

Contents:

Introduction

Pat got it right from the beginning. She was a very deep thinker and wouldn't commit to love until she had thought it through. In a letter to me written just before she went home for Christmas 1968 she wrote, "...On top of this I feel an elusive fondness for you that can't be classified; it's too strong for friendship and not strong enough for love. Whether I will love you in the future, I don't know. I think the chances for it are better than the chances against. I like to think of you and Toronto having a large role to play in my present, & perhaps my future. I would prefer you not to mention marriage again until & unless you feel that I can return your feelings equally. Pat. "

She wanted to be sure we were soulmates. About a month after she got back from Ottawa we were kissing good night after a date when she said, "Eric, I love you!" After recovering from the shock, I replied "Does this mean you will marry me?" She replied "Yes." That was February 9th, 1969 we bought the ring on February 14, 1969 and were married on June 21, 1969.

In this first anniversary poem, she is firmly placing us on the road to becoming the united, eternal resurrection entity mandated by our sacrament of Holy Matrimony.

TO ERIC (21 JUNE 1970)

You love me royally, as I love you,
seated together in our garden Kingdom,
keeping up our silent conversation,
clothed in robes of joy of every hue.
For us, our royal love has had no parallel:
It rooted, grew, and like a miracle
spread to the garden where in now we sit,
Clothed in the fragrance of God in it.

And this long miracle is to discover
the inmost me and you,
to nurse no longing for another,
to forge the soul and its desire together
gently, openly and forever.

Nothing grows but common flowers
outside our Kingdom's wall.
Here alone the magic lies.
We ask nothing; we have all.

Our marriage and love continued to grow stronger and
stronger. Even after death it continues to grow. We are
filling Gods purpose to create a trinity – the unity of Pat, I
and our love into one in God's own image to share in the
creation process. In 1 Corinthians 15:35-54, Paul says,
"The body that is sown is perishable, it is raised
imperishable; it is sown in dishonor, it is raised in glory; it
is sown in weakness, it is raised in power; it is sown a

natural body, it is raised a spiritual body". In short, our resurrected bodies are spiritual, imperishable, and raised in glory and power. Pat dwells in me and I dwell in Pat and we dwell in Christ.

This First Anniversary poem was prophetic. It is so Pat she had to plan everything out before starting it. It is only in the Grief Journey that I got to where she was when we married – God and Us!

The Grief Journey began for me on November 15, 2016, the 48th anniversary of our first date. In her diary entry, the next day Pat wrote: "To my great surprise, I am dying…Huge thud of astonishment – my family usually dies of heart disease! I haven't really recovered – perhaps never will. To Eric it was a terrible blow. Maybe he'll never recover either…."

Pat knows me so well she can ever read my mind. Yes, it was a terrible blow from which I still haven't fully recovered. She knew that the thought of joining her by my own hand had entered my mine; that's why she was especially worried about me. Towards the end she crooked her finger at me and told my not to join her by my own hand and insisted I promise not to, though for the month after her death, January 7th, 2017, I admit it was a very difficult promise to keep.

There are some advantages to being the primary caregiver. I was so busy I didn't have time to think;

though I began the serious prayer journey to God then. It was always about her continuing to dwell in me and my continuing to dwell in her. I was also praying for a remission that would keep her with me a few months longer – I was at the Us and God stage still.

The grief began in earnest at her death. At first it was a sort of numbness. Then came the guilt that I hadn't always been kind and gentle with her during the palliative care period, and that trying to give her water when she couldn't swallow may have drowned her – there was a gaspiness in her breathing before the end. There was also guilt that when she passed I hadn't been beside her holding her hand. She comforted me almost immediately; the next day I felt her presence and her forgiveness. She kissed me. This was the real beginning of her starting me on my journey to God and her.

I started reading her dairies, papers, and journals for the book *Quiet Love…Eyes to see and words to tell the truths that are most true*. This book is a sequel to that book. I also recorded my grief journey on Facebook. What follows are some of those 'posts' with added commentary.

January

Psalm 23 (KJV)

1 The Lord is my shepherd; I shall not want.

2 He maketh me to lie down in green pastures: he leadeth me beside the still waters.

3 He restoreth my soul: he leadeth me in the paths of righteousness for his name's sake.

4 Yea, though I walk through the valley of the shadow of death, I will fear no evil: for thou art with me; thy rod and thy staff they comfort me.

5 Thou preparest a table before me in the presence of mine enemies: thou anointest my head with oil; my cup runneth over.

6 Surely goodness and mercy shall follow me all the days of my life: and I will dwell in the house of the Lord for ever.

January 7, 2017
Pat's Poppa quilt

Pat quilts. The "Poppa" quilt, she herself made from my
old flannel shirts, kept her warm during her palliative
care.
Life is like a Quilt...
Years bound together
Embellished with family
And friends.
Backed with Tradition,
Stitched with Love
With cornerstones placed
carefully
To create a one-of-a-kind
Journey through Time.

Many a Friday night, Vivi and Patricia Bow could be
found under the "Poppa" quilt during happier times – Pat
reading her to sleep.

Pat is still quilting. She is quilting together the separate
pieces of our lives, "...the stumbles of surprise / when,
reaching out in haste, [we found] the stranger self behind
[each other's] eyes.
Thank you everyone who sent cards, letters and phone
calls during her palliative care. Pat is now at peace. If God
choose, I shall but love Pat better after death.

The Church of the Holy Saviour, Anglican reported on January 8 bulletin: Patricia Bow passed away on Saturday night. She had pancreatic cancer and had suffered several strokes. We hold husband Eric and son James and his family: Erin Bow, Vivian and Nora, in our prayers.
The eternal God is thy refuge, and underneath are the everlasting arms. (Deut.33:27)

January 8, 2017
Death is not the extinguishing of the light

Cribbing from my priest on my seeing Pat after I die: Pat is at peace, that same love and peace of God also surrounds and uphold all of us, her family, and all who mourn. Neither death nor any created thing is able to separate us from the divine love we share in a Holy Communion that continues beyond death. Now we see through a glass dimly, but then we shall see clearly face to face. I compare the mystery of death to the mystery and wonder of life itself. Once, we were within the security of the womb and faced the trauma of birth not knowing the awesome wonders nor the love that awaited us in dimensions yet to be experienced. So, shall it be in death. 'Death is not the extinguishing of the light. It is but the putting out of the lamp, for the dawn has come.' and now from E. B. Browning: Patricia, I love thee with the breath, Smiles, tears, of all my life! -- and, if God choose, I shall but love thee better after death. I'll love thee forever.

January 8, 2017
Pooka dies

Just when you think it cannot get any worse you have to
put down your beloved pet. Pooka spent the last two
weeks either on the hospital bed with Pat or sleeping
under it. She was okay when we left for Church this
morning and after we got home from Church but after we
got home from making the funeral arrangements she was
at the top of the stairs crying in pain. We noticed she
couldn't put any weight on her rear left leg. Took her to
emergency services and were told after an x-ray she need
orthopedic surgery and her weak bones (she was 19 and a
½) would not recover well at all. They recommended we
put her down rather than send her to Guelph for the $6000
surgery. Boy the world stinks just now.

January 11, 2017
Patricia BOW Obit

BOW, Patricia The Bow family is sad to announce the
death of Patricia Anne Bow, nee Smith, who died
peacefully on January 7, at home as she wished. Her
battle with pancreatic cancer was brief but difficult. Pat
was a word person to her heart, and some of her own
words tell her story: "My family descended from Scottish,
Irish, and English pioneers who settled in the Ottawa

15

Valley when it was still mostly uncut forest. Family stories infected me with a fascination for history - but above all I loved the hints of adventure and mystery in those tales." She was born in Ottawa in the middle of that big family story, with three older siblings and three younger siblings. All six survive her: Gordon (and Madeline), Dorothy (and her late partner Bruce), Deanna (and the late Dieter), Margaret (and Leon), Bette, and Edward. Chasing her love of history and story, Pat studied history as an undergraduate at Carleton University in Ottawa, then took a graduate degree in library science at the University of Toronto. She wrote: "I love libraries, their richness and generous openness and even their smell." She loved them so much that she married fellow librarian Eric Bow in 1969. Settling in the Bow family home in Toronto's old Chinatown, Eric and Pat had one child, a son, James. Becoming a stay-at-home mother, she raised James into a very fine young man. When James went to university and Eric retired, the family moved to Kitchener-Waterloo. Pat took another degree, this one a diploma in journalism. She worked for the New Hamburg Independent, then joined the University of Waterloo communications office, "where for 12 years I wrote about quantum mechanics and the history of war and peace, and other serious stuff." She retired in 2011, and "decided to go ahead and write what I love to read: fantasy and speculative fiction." Pat's son James married Erin Noteboom in 1998, and in 2005, Pat became a

grandmother, first to Vivian, and then, in 2008, to Nora.
She adored them. The whole Bow family - Eric, James
and Erin, Vivian and Nora - survives Pat, who was only
70. We will remember Pat as sister, wife, and mother and
grandmother, and as the maker of wonderful things: pie
crusts, mittens, stunning quilts. And then of course there
are the books: she wrote and published more than 20
novels, full of ghosts and dragons. Best known, perhaps,
was The Bone Flute, a finalist for the Silver Birch and
Red Cedar Awards. She was a word person but words
cannot express how much we will miss her.

January 11, 2017
Lonely
.

Almighty God, whose Son had nowhere to lay his head:
Grant that those who live alone may not be lonely in their
solitude, but that, following in his steps, they may find
fulfillment in loving you and their neighbors; through
Jesus Christ our Lord. Amen.

January 13, 2017
Pat speaks to me

Yesterday I couldn't find these rings. Last night in a
dream Pat told me where to look for them - specifically
saying the engagement ring was below the friendship ring
and the earrings. Thank you, Patricia Bow, you are still

with me. New meaning to "now we see through a glass darkly" - in my dreams both day and night I see and feel Pat.

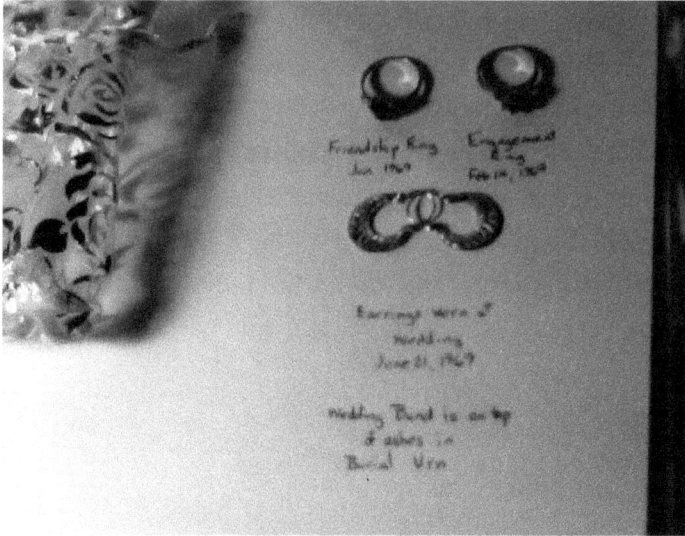

January 15, 2017
Peace I leave you
.

I believe these words yet the tears still keep welling up in my eyes whenever I think of my beloved Pat. Now I see her darkly through a veil and pray for the time when I shall see her again in the Light of Christ.
"Jesus said, "Peace I leave with you; my peace I give you. Do not let your hearts be troubled, and do not let them be afraid." ~ John 14:27"

January 15, 2017
Pat, my morning star

Stars and angels are our Christmas stories and poems.
Father Neil, in The Church of the Holy Saviour Advent
Newsletter, pointed out that Jesus promised his followers
that they too would become morning stars. Pat died on
day one of Epiphany. On that day, Pat rose as the morning
star in my heart. Her message to me is "be not afraid, I am
still with you though now in Heaven." She is preparing
that place Christ promised for us in Heaven, as she
prepared our journey here on earth for happiness. Thank
you, Fr Neil, I receive and share that message; its
assurance indeed brings me peace, now and throughout
the days that lie ahead. Pat, I'll love you forever!
From my Eulogy at Pat's funeral

January 16, 2017
Pat's bucket list

Pat had been planning to repeat our 2003 vacation in
Nova Scotia; it was her dream and on her bucket list. We
bought return tickets on the Atlantic and reserved a
cottage at White Point Beach Motel. We were planning to
go the week of our 48th wedding Anniversary. Cancer is
so cruel.... from diagnosis on the 48th anniversary of our
first date, November 15th, 2016 to her passing away took

only 7 weeks, Pat loved Nova Scotia and walking Nova Scotia's beaches.

January 17, 2017
Pat on diagnosis

.

Pat also wrote this about the pancreatic cancer diagnosis; "Huge thud of astonishment .... I haven't really recovered - perhaps never will. To Eric it was a terrible blow. Maybe he'll never recover either." Patricia Bow really knows me and is right; I don't think I will ever really recover. It is like I have lost half of myself. Pat also wrote: "I hate the fact that I am making several loved people unhappy." and "So much loss, such pain. Please God, please, please, please, please." Well God answered by keeping the pain from her. She died peacefully in her sleep only seven weeks after the diagnosis.
I say "Amen" because this is a prayer.

January 18 ·
Meet again in heaven

Yes, Patricia Bow and I will meet and love again in Heaven. God promises it. "But the answer to whether we'll recognize our departed loved ones now residing in heaven is as certain as our assurance of seeing our Saviour."

January 18, 2017
Why not me

Why Pat and not me? " Men are slightly more likely to
develop pancreatic cancer than women. This may be due,
at least in part, to higher tobacco use in men, which raises
pancreatic cancer risk. The difference in pancreatic cancer
risk was larger in the past (when tobacco use was much
more common among men than women), but the gap has
closed in recent years." I would gladly have died in Pat's
place.

January 19, 2017
A Severe Mercy

S. K. M. F. thought Patricia Bow and I had this same
"sharing" type of marriage as described in Sheldon
Vanauken's "A Severe Mercy'. Having read this last
night, I DO find this could be Pat and I. I am thinking
many of the same things and we lived the same sharing
marriage. Thank you, S.
A Severe Mercy: A Story of Faith, Tragedy and Triumph
by Sheldon Vanauken, C.S. Lewis (Contributor)
4.32 · Rating Details · 10,829 Ratings · 762 Reviews
This acclaimed story traces the idyllic marriage of
Sheldon and Jean Vanauken, their search for faith, their
friendship with C. S. Lewis, and the tragedy of untimely
death and love lost. It includes 18 letters from C. S.

Lewis. Sheldon Vanauken is the author of Gateway to Heaven, The Glittering Illusion, and Under the Mercy, a sequel to A Severe Mercy.
Paperback, 240 pages
Published May 26th, 2009 by HarperOne (first published January 1st, 1977)

January 19, 2017
Seems a lot of people want a gentle death together.
.

When Sheldon Vanauken and his wife become Anglicans, they promise not to die by their own hand. Pat didn't make me promise but she did crook her figure at me and order me not to follow her by my own hand. A very moving passage from Vanauken's book:
"A night or two later, she said to me: "you must hold on to your promise not to follow me, not to die by your own hand." She was, of course, thinking of our old high resolution to go together -- even as I had been thinking of it, haunted by it. The resolution to take Grey Goose [there boat] to sea and sink her. Even now we could still do it. But I said, "I will keep my promise. I will."
"Maybe God will take you," she said, a little hopefully.
"Maybe He will take you at the same moment: that would be sweet."
"I pray He does," I said. "But it will not seem long, if He doesn't."

January 20, 2017
What have I lost

What have I lost: I have lost the ability to enjoy all the
things we enjoyed together; the ability to enjoy every
day's most common loves by sun or candle light. Now I
listen to a piece of music we once enjoyed together and it
sounds hollow. I look at a painting we loved together and
it just doesn't move me in the same way it once did. A
bright sunny day is not appreciated the same. The
atmosphere and food in one of our favourite restaurants
just is not as good anymore. A TV show we both looked
forward to now brings tears to my eyes. The pleasure of
cooking a great meal for supper is gone; it is just food
now. I feel like I have lost half of myself. One exception
is a good BCP service, I feel her presence most strongly
in Church and believe we both are enjoying the service
together. I really want to join her in Heaven; Oh, God let
my release be soon! Amen

January 21, 2017
Pat's love for me

Just came across this declaration of Pat's love for me in
the October 19, 1975 entry:
".... our marriage ... I thought it was getting better &
better, and visualized it getting better indefinitely for the
rest of our lives. I think the stronger you grow in yourself,

the more you can love another person. I can't analyze it very well; in fact, would rather not. Just that more & more, Eric is the only man for me, & without him I would be all in disorganized fragments. If there's a message for him, that's it."
Talk about bringing tears to the eyes.

January 22, 2017
Renaissance woman

Pat was/is a talented, renaissance, woman; I know she loves me as did everyone who saw us interacting together. Yet she kept putting herself down. Here is how she described herself around the 3rd anniversary of our first date (she was 4 months pregnant with James):
"What am I? A third-rate poet, a fourth-rate painter, maybe a second-rate librarian; too muddled to be an intellectual; too reserved to reach out to people effectively; a reluctant house-keeper; a confused Christian. Not pretty enough to have a beautiful woman's self- confidence; sometimes attractive, in many ways plain; deeply in love with my husband, but too self-contained to let it show as much as it might. And yet I am a happy woman. I must have some value as a human being. "

Yes, Pat you have lot of value, look at the number of people you touched and who love you. You are my favourite writer and the best wife any man could have. I think you are beautiful. I'll love you forever.

January 23, 2017
Pat on Death and tombstone inscription

Pat's thoughts in the diary entry of April 5, 1975 didn't change much in the over 27 years to when we made the pre -arrangements. Sure, wish she had made it to at least 75! She (and I) bought a plot, a burial urn and "tombstone" with "Hebrews 1:10-12" inscribed on it on 23/10/2012. She wrote: "It would be amusing to write my own tombstone inscription - something pithy, summing up. Problem is, what I think of me and my life now may be quite different from what I would think of it at the age of, say, 75. Besides, I mean to be cremated -- can you have a tombstone if you're cremated? I firmly believe that when good land is at a premium, it should not be devoted in large quantities to dead people who don't need or appreciate it. Look at Mt Pleasant Cemetery -- acres and acres of lovely parkland, all for the use of dead people. On the other hand, I don't believe in treating our mortal remains casually (though that might be most practical as well as most religious.) I plan to enjoy being in this body for a good many years yet. I like it, for all its faults -- I wouldn't casually trash a favourite pair of shoes, I'd say a little goodbye to them first. Burying the family ashes in a special place in the garden might not be a bad idea. Problem, so many people live in apartments.

January 23, 2017
Pat's ideal place to live

On January 3, 1975, she wrote [After visiting the Royal Winter Fair back in November 1974, we went for a walk along the Lakeshore southeast of Exhibition Place. Here she is thinking back to that walk where we escaped the crowds]

"So, we escaped into the open air. What a relief! We went to walk down by the lake. It was cold, there was no-one else about. On our left was a drab brown park full of trees. On our right was the lake, an infinite expanse of grey water, like rumpled steel. Above, up, in front and behind, was the sky. It was huge, it seemed much higher than I remembered it, and it was full of big dark clouds. They were heavy, very high, too ponderous, like a parade of elephants above our heads.

It was a nice, queer feeling. It made me feel very small, and much calmer. So much space! Immediately I imagined the ideal home: somewhere on a river or lake, not too far out in the wilderness, but not too close to a town either. I saw it sitting large and solid in its grove of trees. Big, warm rooms, big windows you could open to look out into the trees. A big garden. A kind of dark peace over all, at night, and plenty of sunshine in the morning.

So much for that dream!"

[Patricia also wrote the poem "By the Lakeshore" about the park back in 1969; obviously, it was a park we loved to visit,]

January 24, 2017
Pat spared pain

I'm thinking that Someone else was trying to spare Pat the pain I feel now. After all she went through two miscarriages -- 1976 and 1984. It helps me that my surviving (heart attack 2 years ago) spared her the grief and pain I feel now, though it would have been nice to have died peacefully and gently together holding Pat in my arms.

January 25, 2017
Pat concerned about my grief·

Pat's concern over our grief over my mother's death in her diary entry 6-10-1983
"All this while Eric and James were both experiencing more or less complicated degrees of grief (less complicated for Jamie - he just misses his granny) and while I was in a state of tension and watchfulness: watching them, to see who needed company and comfort most....
.... I think these times were the worst for me, knowing how he hurt and unable to help, really, or do anything more useful than hold him."

This is why she asked her sisters to look after me and James and was glad James had Erin by his side. She realized how much I depend on her for comfort. She has always been the stronger emotionally.

January 26, 2017
A sign of her presence

In my post last night, I asked for a sign. Old men frequently visit the W.C. during the night. Twice in the light of the night light on the wall over the tank I saw in Pat's hand dim and faded WRITING ON THE WALL. The third time it was gone but clear in my mind's eye again in Pat's hand.
" I am in Heaven now....
I order you not to join me yet....
I love you Eric forever....
See you in Heaven in time....
I am preparing a place for us...."
Hey, I believe and Pat is helping with my unbelief with the sign I asked for. I don't think grief has made me mad.

January 26, 2017
Pat on death ·

Pat's thoughts about death and the soul have change since she wrote this 6-10-83; she grew in Christ. ".... There is also a kind of confusion about death itself - it's impossible to understand of course. Like a rabbit in a magician's trick. Where did it go? The body remains, but the real woman has vanished! I felt the same after my father's death.

I don't believe that the live soul simply stops existing. It did exist; therefore, it still exists. Where? I suppose one must think in terms of heaven since one must visualize something.

Perhaps it is enough simply to believe the spirit does not die...

January 26, 2017
Pat's Depression

From 26-02-1984 entry in Pat's diary.
"...I think it may be necessary to accept unhappiness as a normal part of life. This idea is really revolutionary for a 20th century North American- we're raised to expect happiness as our birthright, and when bad things happen to us we react with a "Why me?" sense of outraged injustice."
But grief is no respecter of persons. The trick is to avoid making those about you miserable as well. In fact, it is possible to carry sadness as an everyday burden and to go on with normal life at the same time. This is normal life."
Pat is right about this (she wrote it just after her 2nd miscarriage.) but I know she recovered and lived a relatively happy life especially when the granddaughters came.

January 27, 2017
My prayer for Pat

All powerful God,
We pray for thy servant Patricia Bow.
Who responded to the call of Christ
And pursued wholeheartedly the ways of perfect love.
Grant that she may rejoice
On that day when your glory will be revealed
And in the company of all her brothers, sisters, her
husband Eric Bow, her son, her daughter-in-law and her
grand daughters
Share forever the happiness of your Kingdom.
Amen

January 28, 2017
Gillespie visit

Had lovely visit from Paul and Ruth Gillespie. Very nice
to see them again but wished Pat had been there to share
the pleasure. Happens often these days, I'm in tears
because I can't share something pleasant with her. Paul
and Ruth are our oldest friends from the second year of
our marriage.
Ruth Gillespie 'met Jesus on April 21, 2017. Ruth was a
good friend : funny, generous, kind, loving and spent
most of her life caring for others and volunteering.

January 28, 2017
Not the same as spouse going on a trip

When you or your loved one go on a trip you know where
they are and that you'll see them again. You can
communicate with them. When your loved one dies how
is it any different? You know they are in that special place
Christ promised to prepare for believers in Heaven. You
know you will see them again, hold them in your arms. It
is all promised by Christ. Why then does death still hurt
so much? Death has lost its sting. Go to Church, take
Communion and communicate with your loved ones; that
is what the Mass is all about. Your loved one has merely
gone before to prepare a place for you both in Christ's
arms. It will not seem long until God calls you also to his
arms. I believe Oh God help me in my unbelief. Amen.

January 29, 2017
Return to daily routines

.

Return to smallest weekly routine - weekly weighing -
done together, now brings tears to my eyes. I had to weigh
first for some reason; now there is no second person to be
weighed
I have no ugly images of the death of Pat. She died
peacefully and I remember how beautiful and peaceful
she looked, just like she was sleeping. In fact, I thought
she was sleeping and tried to wake her. We had a

beautiful marriage - there are NO dark images. I loved her very much; with great love comes great pain but it is NOT ugly.

January 29, 2017
Basic – her love poem to me

.

Wow I always knew Pat loved me and she felt our marriage was getting better all the time and would continue forever. I just found this love poem she wrote for me 1975. Talk about bringing tears to the eye.
Basic
by Patricia A. Bow Easter 1975
I love you little more than I love air
for every time I draw a breath
a puff withstands the void of death:
I love you little more than I love air.

I love you little more than I love water.
It sends the new green springing high,
without it I would surely die;
I love you little more than I love water.

I love you little more than I love bread.
It binds the muscle to the bone,
it sends the heartbeat throbbing on;
I love you little more than I love bread.

I now recite it to her ever day, adding my own last verse:

I love you little more than I love life
For it made us man and wife,
Together in unity for all eternity.
I love you little more than I love life.

January 31, 2017
Comments on little memories.
.

W. N. wrote "And the little things will trigger memories
for the rest of your life."
I replied "Kind of hope it won't be too long before I join
her in Heaven. Pat was three score and ten but I am
strong. The days of our years are threescore years and ten;
and if by reason of strength they be fourscore years, yet is
their strength labour and sorrow; for it is soon cut off, and
we fly away."
I will love Pat forever.

February

A valentine Sonnet to E____
By Patricia A. Bow (1970)

Beside the roses in this red bouquet
Accept the thoughts of flowers I could not buy
Sprays of mezereum to please you by,
Peach blossoms, cedar leaves, that try to say
Why crocuses mean much to me today.
Rampant amongst the others, stretching high.
The rose and myrtle twine in one great sigh,
Now serious, now bending down to play.
Humble but constant, bay leaves down below
Express in fragrance what cannot be said.
Eager and bright, the coxcomb flowers grow
And bring the vital question to a head:
Just answer yes, and give me mistletoe;
Then shall the roses bloom forever red.

February 1, 2017
 Special place in heaven

Remember my "You know they are in that special place
Christ promised to prepare for believers in Heaven. You
know you will see them again, hold them in your arms. It
is all promised by Christ. Why then does death still hurt
so much? Death has lost its sting." post? Well I've got the
answer and it's all about time. Alive we are in time while
Pat is in eternity. We want comfort now; for Pat, there is
NO now she is in Eternity - an eon is little more than a
second. We are used to instant gratification and want
everything NOW! Hey, that is, why Simeon (St. Luke
2.22.) says "Lord, now lettest thou thy servant depart in
peace. According to thy word; for mine eyes have seen
thy salvation, which thou hast prepared before the face of
all people. I'm no different than Simeon I want to hold
and talk to Pat NOW and join her in Heaven NOW.

February 2, 2017
Pat's apple pie for my birthday

Pat, at my request, used to make me an apple pie (1/2
Macs 1/2 Ida Reds) with a butter pastry crust for my
birthday. Sure, wish I could visit her in our place in
heaven this birthday for a slice of that pie I know she
would have it ready! Pat, I love you forever.!

February 6, 2017
After my birthday

Yes, my birthday without Pat for the first time in 48 years, was hard. But, this morning is even worse; I am all teary and really hurting.

Found this good advice: "The death of a spouse is one of the most traumatic events a person can experience in life. It's easy to understand why you might be feeling terribly lonely. You may even be wrestling with serious spiritual questions and doubts. Sleepless nights and the pressure of sudden responsibilities can take a huge toll on your reserves of physical and mental energy at a time like this. Routine things may seem to take more effort. Our hearts go out to you during this period of grief and readjustment. The important thing at this point is to give yourself time and space to grieve. You may even want to set aside an hour every day or so to "work" on your grief. As you go through this process, remember that God loves you more than you realize. He is there to help if you'll reach out to Him. He understands your loneliness and hurt. He is more than willing to meet your needs. Our prayer is that you will sense His presence and know the peace that surpasses all understanding as you move through this dark valley." Still praying along with Simeon in Luke, "Lord, now let thy servant depart in peace." I love Pat forever and look

forward to God bringing us together in our place in
Heaven promised by Christ.

February 6, 2017
Should have been me

There may be another reason God did not take me before
Pat and it may not be because He had a special plan for
me. Pat was the better half, the stronger and the better
Christian. I on the other hand: I may still have something
to atone for before I can join her in Heaven. This is what
comes of brooding. I believe, God help me in my
unbelief.

February 7, 2017
Support of our priest

Pat and I were very much upheld by the prayers of Fr Neil
and of our parish family during the seven weeks of
palliative care from Diagnose to her passing. If I forgot to
thank you all for the support and prayers, I apologize and
do so now. She was particularly helped by this Bible
reading suggested by Fr Neil, Philippians 4:8 (KJV) [I
just found now on her bulletin board]
"Finally, brethren, whatsoever things are, true, whatsoever
things are honest, whatsoever things are just, whatsoever
things are pure, whatsoever things are lovely, whatsoever
things are of good report; if there be any virtue, and if
there be any praise, think on these things."

February 7, 2017
Pat on death

Found on Pat's computer, file is dated November 22, 2016
a week after she found out she was dying:
"Death is not extinguishing the light; it is only putting out
the lamp because the dawn has come."
— Rabindranath Tagore
It is so Pat!

February 7, 2017
Loving Pat after death

They say absence makes the heart grow fonder. Meaning
– We will feel more affection for someone when we are
not with them. Pat is in our special place in Heaven. Great
love means great pain. So, the pain of my grief will only
grow not lessen and I shall but love Pat better after death!
February 8, 2017
Christ on cross

And about the ninth hour Jesus cried with a loud voice,
saying, Eli, Eli, lama sabachthani? that is to say, My God,
my God, why hast thou forsaken me?

"Yet all the griefs he felt were ours,
Ours were the woes he bore;
Pangs, not his own, his spotless soul

With bitter anguish tore.
"We held him as condemn'd of heaven,
An outcast from his God;
While for our sins he groaned, he bled,
Beneath his Father's rod."

February 8, 2017
Pat waiting
.

When Pat was in the hospital the first time (mobile and
not in isolation), I spent every day at her bedside from
8:30 am to 8:30 pm (did the same the other two times but
she was not allowed out of her room.) There was one
morning I was late and I found her waiting by the
elevators for me when I got off. Pat didn't like being
alone; oh, there were times during the day Pat wanted to
be alone on walks but never at night, particularly at night.
She wrote " I think I could live fairly contentedly through
any crisis that might come, as long as I know I can depend
on his [that's me] presence." She also wrote "I do need my
time alone .... but I keep telling myself the day may come
when I will be alone - all alone." I wonder when it comes
my time to join her if she'll be waiting for me at the Gates
of Heaven? Lord now let thy servant depart in peace so I
can join her in our place in Heaven.
February 8, 2017
My prayer for joining Pat

MOST merciful Father, who hast been pleased to take
unto thyself my beloved wife, Patricia Bow, departed:
Grant to us who are still in our pilgrimage, and who walk
as yet by faith, that having served thee faithfully in this
world, we may, with all faithful Christian souls, be joined
hereafter to the company of thy blessed Saints in glory;
through Jesus Christ our Lord, who with thee and the
Holy Spirit liveth and reigneth, one God, world without
end. Amen.

It is my hope and belief that Pat as a member of the
company of thy blessed Saints can hear me and
communicate with me most readily during the Holy
Communion Service. I'm so glad Fr Neil gives us an few
minutes of silence before the formal prayers begin (on
Wednesday mornings only) during which I can speak to
Pat. It is why I have started going Wednesdays as well as
Sundays.

February 9, 2017

Pat and I joined

Since Pat and I did everything together
and are "joined together by God" and Christ himself said
of husband and wife, "Wherefore they are no more twain
but one flesh." how come her journey on earth is complete
and mine is still not done? Okay Lord, what have I left
undone which I ought to have done; And what have I
done which I ought not to have done. When will I
complete my tasks and see salvation and when can I

repeat Simeon's "Lord, now let thy servant depart in peace for I have seen thine salvation'?

February 9, 2017
More grief

VERY STRANGE MOOD CAME UPON ME: Picked up Pats slippers from top of stairs and put them in the closet. Suddenly I was overwhelmed by grief, tears and a desire to be dead it was so bad I couldn't bear it. It almost caused me to blackout but I went on as if I was a robot doing the Thursday garbage night chores. This is after another strange phenomenon last evening: I had been napping and when I opened my eyes I saw Pat's poetry quite clearly scrolling before my eyes on brown paper and some of her diary entries. They scrolled slowly enough for me to actually read some of them and they were new not what I have been reading for the project. I have no idea what is happening to me. I don't take any drugs that would cause this and otherwise I seem sane. Any ideas friends and family on Facebook?

February 10, 2017
Pat's last writings

.

Pat's diary entry dated Sun. Dec. 4 in very shaky hand writing " "Started as a dull day but improved with visitors - Eric, James, Dani, Fr Neil. Also, I have CDS + audio books. Very hard to read since can't see well - vision disturbance". I'm convinced this and the really bad headaches with rainbows around small stars in her vision range from end of October to end of December were "silent strokes" and they are what brought on her end. I've been told nobody dies from cancer they die from its complications. Cancer sucks!

February 11, 2017
Boy, do I ever relate to this:

"She was not only my wife. She was also the one who would tell me if my socks matched; if my tie was straight, or if my hair was combed. She was able to tell me with one look if I was talking too much or saying something stupid. She was the one who would remember all the birthdays and special occasions, and all I had to do was sign cards. She was good at all the things I am not good at. So, she complemented me and made me more whole. God, I miss her so much. I feel like part of me is missing."

February 11, 2017
Jesuit thoughts

"Listen to your heart, your longings, the pain you experience when you can find no meaning in life. Keep asking yourself: 'Basically, what do I long for more than anything?' Keep asking this question." [from Jesuits in

44

Britain post] The answer is God's plan for you. So, if my strongest desire is to join Pat in the Heavenly place Christ promised to prepare for us that is God's plan for me. I can pray along with Simeon: "Lord now let thy servant depart in Peace to join my beloved in Heaven" Particular if I add Christ's own words "not my well but Thine."

February 12, 2017
Need quiet company

What I need most is quiet company. I just need someone to sit with me, to grieve with me....no words, no advice... just someone to be with me, to sit in silence and be there beside me as I cry internally and pray "Lord now let thy servant depart in Peace to join my beloved wife, Pat, in the place in Heaven promised by Christ."

February 12, 2017
Sunday routines – Vinyl Cafe

Every Sunday after Church Pat and I had this ritual: I would buy Zehr's 5 wing combo; she would make herself a grilled cheese sandwich and tea for two. We'd get comfortable and turn on CBC Radio to listen to the Vinyl Cafe. Well today after Church I made myself a grilled cheese in Pat's memory and turned on the CBC - NO Vinyl Cafe! Starting in January 2017, we won't be airing The Vinyl Cafe on CBC Radio, Stuart was diagnosed with melanoma a year ago. At the time, we figured the treatment would be swift. What can I say … things don't always go exactly as planned? Cancer sucks! I am very sad now both for Pat and Stuart and the Vinyl Cafe.

February 12, 2017
Counting our blessings:

Thinking about our 48 years together I realise we really had a beautiful happy marriage. Yes, this is absolutely true: "Patricia and I were lucky enough to discover that quiet, intense love that is basic to life itself; it is seldom found in real life. We had the eyes to see and the words to tell the truths that are most real to each other." O there were stresses and tensions but nothing serious. Pat achieved what she wanted above all else: to be a published author. We have a son with whom we are well pleased and two gorgeous granddaughters with whom we are also well pleased. The last 10 years were perfect since pensions and benefit packages meant we had no financial worries and were relatively well off. We had even planned and paid for a return to Nova Scotia the REAL holiday Pat and I so wanted. Pat's departure was in Peace in her sleep with none of the pain she so feared and she died at home where she wanted to die. She is in Heaven now waiting for me in our place in Heaven Christ promised. Okay I'm feeling real pain but by not being called first I spared Pat this pain. Only thing that could have made things really perfect would have been dying together hand in hand asleep in our bed. But it was not to be and now I wait in pain to join her in Heaven. Surely, I can't be criticized for not waiting patiently on God's will or plan for me and praying daily that God take me now to join Pat in Heaven. Even Christ on the cross prayed for death though He added "Not my will but Thine."

February 13, 2017
Sure, of Pat's presence

After reading Tom Harper's Life after Death, Pat wrote "interesting and providing food for thought, especially on the question of the resurrection of the body. Off and on I've thought about ageing and dying, and I really don't think I'll enjoy it "
I wonder if what I saw January 26/27, twice on the wall over the toilet tank, in Pat's hand: ...
" I am in Heaven now....
I order you not to join me yet....
I love you Eric forever....
See you in Heaven in time....
I am preparing a place for us...."
...was her attempt to tell me dying wasn't really all that bad? It certainly is telling me that she is in Heaven waiting and I am equally sure it wasn't an Hallucination or dust on the wall (I tried to wipe it off with toilet paper.)

47

February 13, 2017
Husband wife united as one

.

The relationship between a husband and wife is different
from all other family relationships. In no other case does
God join two into one. When you lose a spouse you really
do lose half of yourself and a big hole is left inside you.
Now Pat died soon after reaching three score and 10; I am
strong so am expected to reach four score. That thought
fills me with horror; I really don't want to live 6 more
years without my other half. But Lord, Thine will not
mine.

February 14, 2017
My Valentine

To my beloved wife in Heaven, Happy Valentine's Day!
48th anniversary of Engagement!

Why is it the only person I want hugs and comfort from
today, my beloved wife Patricia, is strangely silent. Lord
now let Thy servant's cry reach his wife in Heaven in that
place that Christ promised. Let me have ears to hear her
speak her love for me and words to tell her "Pat I love you
forever! Oh, God forsake me not.

February 15, 2017
On Matrimony

.

Matrimony is an honourable estate instituted of God signifying the mystical union between Christ and His Church.

He answered, "Have you not read that he who created them from the beginning made them male and female, and said, 'Therefore a man shall leave his father and his mother and hold fast to his wife, and the two shall become one flesh'? So, they are no longer two but one flesh. What therefore God has joined together, let not man separate." Mathew 19:4-6

Since Christ vanquished Death we are one flesh and a united soul forever. The ring symbolises Eternity!

February 15, 2017
Stronger presence

Something has changed! I am now aware of my wife, Patricia's presence touching me. Started last night and grew stronger at Mass this morning (sat beside a retired well loved priest). It is as if we are made whole again; Oh, I still miss her physical presence and her words and tears still come at small memories. But she is there with me her presence and her spiritual strength comfort and support me. Surely, we shall dwell united in the house of the Lord forever.

February 17 ·
On touching

The truth is, the best marriages engage in a lot of touching, and sex is only one form of touching. Now this is a problem when your loved one is in Heaven and you are on earth. Jesus saith unto her, touch me not; for I am not yet ascended to my Father: but go to my brethren, and say unto them, I ascend unto my Father, and your Father; and to my God, and your God. Pat's resurrected spiritual body is with God; even though our two souls are as one here on earth. There is no physical touching only dreams of such. That is why I still feel lonely. But there will come a time when we are together in heaven and neither of us will be sad or lonely ever again. In the meantime, spiritual touching, like what you feel when you take the bread and the wine at Communion, is very comforting!

February 18, 2017
Communion

.

A truth I've discovered: In the absence of physical touching with a loved one, spiritual touching, like what you feel when you take the bread and the wine at Communion, is very comforting! I kiss her portrait morning and night and greet her with "Good morning Love" and "Good night Pat, love you forever!" - it is like taking the bread and the wine at Mass, the portrait and the kiss are very real signs of Pat's presence in a way surpassing understanding. And just as in the Mass her real presence is within me

February 19, 2017
Still miss the physical Pat

.

Still missing Pat's words and laughter; spiritual presence is not the same as having her share a physical joy. When it comes right down to it the house is awfully empty without another physical person in it. Still praying "Lord now let Thy servant depart in Peace to join his wife in Heaven - but not my will but Thine. Amen."

February 19 ·, 2017
Pat's place

Pat wrote during a lovely summer day: " I came for a walk by myself and I am sitting in the little Canadian garden near Shepherd School - lovely little place. The breeze feels like the movement of water, swimming outdoors on a hot day - cool on the skin, soft, smelling of organic things. I wish summer could last forever." ....
AND I want to ask her: "In Heaven, does Summer last forever, are there even seasons in Heaven (I suspect not)." This is the earthly, physical self feeling lonely in an empty house; one feels a need for actual physical conversation with your loved one in Heaven.

February 20, 2017
On loneliness

What do you do when loneliness becomes too much to bear? As an only child who also is the child of an alcoholic mother I experienced loneliness at a very young age. But now I have been with Pat for over 48 years. We were very seldom apart and when we were there was the telephone. Okay we commune in spirit but it is still hard. I miss the words, the physical touch and yes, the sight of her here beside me. All I can do is pray with Simeon "Lord now let Thy servant depart in Peace to join my beloved wife Patricia Bow in that place in heaven Christ promises." Amen. And Pat, I am adding "Not my will but Thine!" as per your crooked finger. Loneliness hurts - are we sure it is not Hell?

February 21, 2017
Acquire a new cat, Piper

Hey, I adopted a small timid 2-year-old female cat named "Piper." That should help with the emptiness of the house and the loneliness. James was with me and agreed that if God should answer my prayer to let me depart now to join Pat in our place in Heaven then he would make a place in his house for Piper.

February 21, 2017
Love is stronger than Death

"Maybe God will take you," she said hopefully. "Maybe
He will take you a little after me: that would be sweet." "I
pray He does, " I said. "But it will not seem long, if He
doesn't." "God's will be done!" - Sheldon Vanauken.
"This is my body given for you..." May Pat and I be to
one another as Christ is to us." So, what does Christ mean
to me? Everything. Love is stronger than DEATH"

February 22 at 7:58am
Pat on Purgatory
.

Wow found this rather disturbing [did she want to die?]
entry by Pat for New Year's Eve 2009: "...at 2020... Eric
and I will be indisputably old or maybe we'll be dead by
then. [she predicted true for her so I've only got only three
more years] ...I really do hope there is a purgatory, or, as
Lewis depicts it, a time of journeying, after death, because
my soul needs a lot more work before it can come to
heaven, if ever it does. Perhaps that's the liberation I can
look forward to, the "Me" falling away, finally. How do
you live, day to day, when you're stuck in the same body
with a person you mostly dislike and despise? Because no
amount of well-intentioned action, good works,
kindnesses, courtesy, honourable conduct, honesty, can
change the real person underneath. Still, you can try, I

suppose that will be my resolution for 2010: to do something every day that a better person would have done naturally, without thinking. A drop of grace in the sea of unredemed selfishness." So, glad she's in the arms of Christ, she desperately needs comforting!

In as much as Pat and I became one flesh by our marriage and are no longer two but one flesh. I am praying the following as that united one soul, hoping to reach across the divide as she does to me from the other side to comfort her in her distress over being unworthy. " Almighty and everliving God, here we offer and present unto thee, O Lord, ourselves, our souls and bodies, our union, to be a reasonable, holy, and living sacrifice unto thee. And although we are unworthy, yet we beseech thee to accept this our bounden duty and service, not weighing our merits, but pardoning our offences; through Jesus Christ our Lord, to whom, with thee and the Holy Ghost, be all honour and glory, world without end. Amen

February 23 at 5:02pm
Life lacks luster

.

After the loss of a spouse, everything in your life loses much of its luster and meaning; you find even those chores that were essential to maintaining your love nest are incredibly mundane and boring. Yet they hold enough memories to bring on the tears when you do get around to doing them. You walk around in a daze not wanting to do them. Hey, they are NOT part of God's plan for you so why do them? Besides I don't think God has a plan for each of us. He gave us Free Will and God seeing what we will do in the future neither negates this free will nor points to Him having a plan for us. What will be will be as the old song says. You feel the spiritual presence of your beloved but crave more - a kiss, a word, a physical touch. You are the earthly half of the two souls made one and very lonely. Life here on earth is without meaning and colourless. You cannot be blamed for praying "Lord, now let Thy servant depart in Peace to join his beloved wife in Heaven". BUT you are forgetting that wanting to die, though not a sin as even Christ prayed for death, is hurtful to those loved ones here on earth. Pat realized this, when she expressed regret at hurting those she loved the most and crooked her finger at me ordering me NOT to join her by my own hand. She also knew and said as much when she said, "I don't know if Eric will ever get over it," I don't know either. On New Year's Day, 2010 Pat predicted she and I would not see 2020; well she was right about herself - and I kind of hope she is right about me. Sorry all! I can't help it. We all handle GRIEF in our own way and there is no right or wrong way to grieve.

February 24, 2017
The Lord is my shepherd

"Yea, though I walk through the valley of the shadow of death, I will fear no evil; for thou art with me; thy rod and thy staff, they comfort me" (Psalm 23:4). Pat often, even at Tai Chi, recited the 23rd psalm to herself and found it comforting. One of the hymns she chose for her Funeral is based on this psalm. I am now depending on His guidance to lead me out of that dark valley I seem to have dug myself into. I believe both Pat and I will dwell in the house of the Lord forever. And I shall love Pat forever!

February 25, 2017 at 9:29am
Shift from personal care to grief

.

When the person we love or care about dies, the emphasis suddenly shifts from caring for her to grief at her loss. I am trying to counteract this by prayers and psalms for Patricia. I have read the depression, doubt and inferiority she expressed in her diaries. I am trying to take away that pain she endured during those decades of self doubt and those tears I saw in her eyes this Christmas and during her last three days with those comfort poems I have been posting - they are NOT about me but are for Pat. I know she is in Heaven but there is also half her soul still with me - we were made one soul but still two persons by marriage. That soul can benefit from her favourite biblical words of comfort from the Mass and the psalms. This is not to deny my need to grieve nor the very real sense of

suffering that I am experiencing from her loss, it's just
that I truly want my beloved wife, Patricia, to be happy

February.25, 2017
Holding her hand

I really regret I wasn't holding Pat's hand when she passed
now and truly at Peace. Pat, I love you forever!
She passed somewhere between 5:15 pm and 6:45 pm on
January 7, 2017. I know between 6:30 and 6:45 I was on
the phone one room away trying to guide a new PSW
worker to my house. Between 5:15 and 6:30 I could have
been anywhere - mostly in either the computer room or
the kitchen. I know how special it is to hold her hand as
she passed. Even though by that last day she was not
responding to anything it was important to me that she
knew I was there. Fortunately, she repeatedly says in her
dairies that she was always aware I was around even
when not in the same room. I still feel a bit guilty. Pat I'm
so sorry! I love you forever. Now this one is for me -
"Please Pat and Lord! forgive, help, and comfort me!"
Amen. PS I take great relief in fulfilling her wish to died
at home!

February 26, 2017 at 8:44pm
Dinner at son's place
Lovely dinner at James and Erin's with the
granddaughters too. I brought the dessert - a lovely apple

pie baked by K. Y. Thank you, Karen, somebody reads my posts - very thoughtfully remembering on my birthday my missing Pat's famous birthday apple pie.

February 27, 2017 at 9:30am ·
Experiencing her presence

In fact, I have had three experiences of communicating with Pat after she departed. On the day, immediately after I was napping on the couch, I was alone in the house. I woke to someone kissing me on the lips like we so often kissed good night. It was Pat or her spirit who dissolved into air as I became more fully awake.
Also see my Facebook entry on January 28th and the one on February 16, 2017.
So yes, I shall see Pat again. I am in fact feeling her presence as I type this. It becomes more present and clearer if I empty my mind as in meditation. I am as sure of this as I am of anything on earth or Heaven. I go around the house talking to her even though I know spiritual communication is not in words but in feelings and minds touching - that is why we meditate in the first place to get in touch with God.
So, we are no longer two but one and "till death do us part" is no longer relevant. Since Christ vanquished Death we are one and a united soul forever. The ring symbolises Eternity!

February 27, 2017 at 3:28 pm
She is still in me

I am now aware of my wife Patricia's presence touching my mind and soul for a couple of weeks now. It is as if we are made whole again. Maybe we never separated. Pat is definitely in my soul almost as if we are sharing one mind. When I'm not using my mind fully (as when I first wake or when I'm falling asleep), I seem to see what Pat is seeing - what she is writing. It is so clear that often I can read it. Those who know Pat, know that writing was all she wanted to do; it was her compulsion. Her idea of Heaven would be a place where she could write without interruption. I feel she is happy now beyond measure writing in our place in Heaven.

February 27, 2017 at 7:14pm ·
On Lewis' "A Grief Observed

Just finished C.S. Lewis' "A Grief Observed" and I am in tears. Why would a description of what I'm going though bring me to tears? Lewis' beliefs about death and God are not mine; but they are close enough to make me cry. We come to the same conclusion - there is life after death and our beloved is there comforting us on our journey to join her.

February 28, 2017 at 5:45am ·
On Vanauken's "A Severe Mercy."

In A Severe Mercy C. S. Lewis in a letter to Vanauken
about 'a life so wholly (at first) devoted to us'; "So from
US you have been led back to US AND GOD; it remains
to go onto GOD AND US. She was further on than you,
and she can help you more where she is than she could
have done on earth. You must go on. That is one of the
many reasons why suicide is out of the question. (Another
is the absence of any ground for believing that death by
that route would reunite you with her. Why should it?
You might be digging an eternally unbridgeable chasm.
Disobedience is not the way to get nearer to the
obedient.)" [I would add Vanauken is already united with
her in God - her half in heaven, his half on earth are
united in and through the arms of Christ.]

February 28, 2017 at 9:44am ·
Dreams of Pat

Had a dream - a bad one - that woke me at 4 am.
Interpreting the dream, I find that my subconscious is
angry with Pat for leaving me to search for God, may
even be jealous of God. However, at the end of the dream,
Pat and I were reconciled and looking for our place in
Heaven. Maybe we have reached C. S. Lewis' US AND
GOD stage. Not angry or jealous now. Images: Ottawa

(our capital) = heaven, new hair style and shiny makeup = new spiritual body, divorce = death, search for job = search for purpose and God, Search for apartment = search for our place in Heaven, etc. Boy our minds are complicated places. Pat used to do this with her dreams so I figure she is helping me now. Pat, I love you now and forever.

February 28, 2017 at 10:16am
Photos

Unlike C. S. Lewis I have lots of photographs of my beloved Pat and they help me focus my mind on her. I have one in every room of the house - some printed, framed and installed after she died 7 weeks ago. The one over her night table in the bedroom is the most important - it's the one I kiss and say, "good morning" to and just before bed kiss and say, "Pat I love you forever!" just as I did for 48 years. Okay they have become icons I talk to and it comforts me greatly. They can turn me at any moment to a whimpering child. But that is a good thing; I never want that hole in my heart ever to be filled; it is the scar of a great love. Pat, I love you, forever.

March

THE MADILL SETTLEMENT
Feb.2/87   April 4/92

These weathered walls, silvery
and porous as old bones
lie still unburied in the wood

though year by year the forest tries
with warp of grass
and weft of mould
to weave a shroud.

Flesh to dust, wood to forest.
here, too many claims conflict.

Wind cries through glassless windows, broken doors:
"Your forefathers forsook us and we died."

Yielding the claim of blood
I join the vigil for an hour
to listen for the creak of iron shod wheels.

March 1, 2017 at 8:14am ·
Pat my treasure in heaven
Matthew 6:21 For where your treasure is, there your heart
will be also.

My treasure is Pat and she is in Heaven - she is also in my
heart!

Jesus reminds us that our hearts follow and give
themselves to what we treasure. Sure, hope my life is
headed in the direction of joining Pat in our place in
Heaven. Joining Pat in Heaven is certainly what occupies
my thoughts and worries. I have named my treasures, and
found what is in my heart. I'm not giving them up for
Lent. I hope to reach C. S. Lewis' GOD AND US stage.

March 1, 2017 at 10:32am ·
True Love/soul mates

What does it mean to be truly in love? In a nutshell, our
quiet, sharing love was a spiritual union of souls: two
individuals united before God but still separate, different
individuals. We respected each other's privacy but were
still touching. We were always aware of each other's
presence even when we were not in the same room. Ours
was/is a union between soul mates. Pat wrote " I do need
my time alone (I don't think he does) but I keep telling
myself the day may come when I will be alone -- all
alone. And I won't like it. I'm sure the nights would be the

worst..." Well that time never came for her - it came for me, it came for me, and the nights ARE the worse.

March 1, 2017 at 12:45pm ·
BCP Ash Wednesday service

For the past decade, Pat and I have been searching for a FULL BCP Ash Wednesday service. Just one of her complaints: Wednesday March 5 2014.... then went to church at 7, for the Ash Wednesday service. It's unfortunate that there seems to be no convenient places to go for a BCP service. Parts of this were good, sombre, powerful, effective - the Penitential Litany. Other parts - the BAS version of Eucharistic prayers especially, were jarring, the language clunky, the music kindergartenish.

Don't know why I forget, every year, how this treatment of the service angers me. I know it shouldn't, but it just rubs me entirely the wrong way.

It's doubly annoying because there is a perfectly good Ash Wednesday service in the BCP which I will now go and read.

Well TODAY ASH WEDNESDAY 2017, Fr. Carver gave Pat the greatest gift: a full Ash Wednesday BCP service. I could feel Pat's pleasure inside me - she saw and heard it through my eyes and ears. Thank you, Fr. Carver, Pat also thanks you.

March 4, 2017 at 9:03am
Not ready yet

It just occurred to me, that those who pray, "Lord take me for I am ready" aren't really ready. If they were, they would feel Christ within them and hear Him speaking directly to them. They would not be their usual self but an eternal self. And if it is a spouse they are seeking to rejoin, they would realise that they are already joined. Of the bodies that held and touched and comforted and stood by each other in anger and despair, one has died so that her strength could be in him. They are now to one another, as Christ is to them. The earthly spouse would feel the beloved eternal spouse there in the bread and wine with Christ. Then maybe if it is God's will, the earthly spouse would truly be ready to depart in peace to be once again, made whole into one Heavenly body with their beloved in that place Christ promised. I believe this is what C. S. Lewis meant by GOD AND US.

Tuesday March 4, 2017 at 7:30
Pat is closest at her computer

Yesterday Pat communicated to me that she was closest when she was at her computer. Okay, when she was alive she was happiest either writing in her journal, notebook, diary or on her computer. Her main computer is next to mine; today I don't think she was referring to it. These days, she often gets her message through by letting me see what she is typing on what looks like a FB screen. I think she has created a mental computer in her Resurrection body and this is the one she means in yesterday's message.

Tuesday March 4, 2017 at 10:15
Real Image of Pat

C. S. Lewis' fear that the real image of his wife, Joy, would be replaced by his memories of her changed by what he wanted her to have been or remembered her to have been without the parts that he didn't want – she'd become an idealized image. The real Joy was no longer there as a reference point to ensure accuracy. He feared instead of loving the real her he would be loving his image of her and it would be more him than her. When you think about it, it probably explains why Christ gave His followers the Mass. "Do this in remembrance of me" and further instructed them to do this as oft as they gathered together in his memory. The Mass ensures both a collective more accurate memory and evokes the real presence of Christ as a reference point. You can't go far wrong if you have the presence of Christ correcting you. I think that Lewis has raised a real danger for many people on the grief journey. The pain makes them remember only the good and the image of their loved one gradually becomes idealized and no longer accurate. It could happen to me as well. Already I find it difficult to visualize her in my mind (without the aid of photos) or remember ALL of her as she was in the last few months. It is why I appreciated her dairies when I put together Quiet Love. In the early part of the journey, grief seems to throw a blanket over you that clouds out everything.

In some of my posts I occasionally have let my image of Pat speak. But when I go too far from who she really was/is her presence corrects me. She gets crotchety on that screen she types to me on and the words flow very fast. Pat snaps at me about what I wrote and she corrects me or tells me not to dare to write about that. I am reminded that she is much more than the she who lives in my memory. She is not dead, she is risen and in the loving arms of Christ and partly in me. C. S. Lewis wrote "The most precious gift that marriage gave me was this constant impact of something very close and intimate yet all the time other, resistant – in a word, real." Lewis rejects that the two made one of the marriage sacrament, continues for all eternity.

The problem of not confusing the memory Pat with the Real presence Pat could also be in me; but, isn't because I believe Love is stronger than Death. Thank God for her corrections, scolding, reassurances and declarations of love and for her very real presence. I can feel her approval when I get something right and her anger when I get something wrong because of that presence. I am in love with the Real her and unlike Lewis I don't have to worry about falling in love with my created image of Pat.

I don't need an graven image of Pat, in the Real presence of her in me I have the real thing.

She IS at peace now. At her death, she was taken directly into the arms of Christ and into that peace that passeth all understanding. Every time she communicates with me I can feel that peace in her. Unfortunately, I don't seem to share that peace yet, even though I feel her presence in me. I still feel lonely and still cry for proof and comfort with mad endearments and entreaties spoken to her and God. Lord I believe help me in my unbelief. Amen

March 7, 2017 at 2:15pm ·
Grief

Grief is like a yoyo. It keeps coming back to hit you in the face. Feel better for days then you pull some string connected to the past and back it comes.

March 8, 2017 at 8:24am
Our marriage

Pat's 12th Anniversary Poem pretty much sums up our marriage. We were so much together people couldn't tell "which is which, and whose is whose." We are still intertwined - I here, her in heaven. Pat, I love you forever.

March 8, 2017 at 10:41am ·
Communicating with Pat

Napping again. Saw through Pat's eyes again. She was reading and typing on what looked a lot like Facebook. I'm pretty sure Facebook isn't in heaven. Maybe one communicates in heaven using copies of your favourite method of communicating on earth. Pat was a written word person, so maybe... Or she is reading what her loved ones' type here on earth and responding in a form of dream to that loved one. James, you any experiences of seeing what Pat sees as you dream?

March 8, 2017 at 3:20pm ·
Hole in my heart

We are entwined forever - me on earth she in heaven. Love is stronger than death. I love her little more than I love life itself. See her poem "Basic." Neither of us want to be "freed." I want that hole in my heart to last till Pat and I meet again in heaven and God heals us.

March 9, 2017 at 9:52am
Being physically alone
.

Grief is an odd thing. Pat is in Heaven in the arms of Christ and happy and comforted; I am here on earth, OK, sharing some of that comfort though continued Communion with He and her. BUT, I am resentful too at being alone and jealous she is in paradise while I still have to wait. I am also happy for her You can be happy for someone and jealous at the same time. Am I committing a sin? "Thou shall not covet your neighbour's house." Maybe it is allowed since when I get there it will also be the place Pat prepared for us and I'll be happy too. So, there you have it.

March 10, 2017 at 6:14pm ·
Pat approves

I'm getting vibes from Pat that she likes both Quiet Love Memoir and Quiet Love the Poems. In fact, for days, now I been getting the message from Pat, that I had missed one poem in the memoir. I couldn't find it. Well today while producing "The Poems" I found it - two pages of her poem notebook were stuck together. Wow Pat is aware of what I'm doing and I feel she approves. Kudos to LULU too - I put together The Poems and Lulu had it up online ready for ordering in less than 4 hours!

March 10, 2017 at 11:10pm
Handling grief

Thank you all for your concern and suggestions I join a Grief group. I am an only child and grew up often alone. I don't always need company. You need to be alone to meditate and I learned to meditate in my teens. I understand how being alone puts you in contact with yourself. These days it puts me in contact with both her and Christ. Please also remember, like Pat I'm not comfortable in groups or parties; Pat and I were the people you see sitting in some corner uncomfortably watching the other guests socialising. Pat actually wanted a hermit's life with me and her - she didn't get it that you can't be a hermit with your spouse present. We also did not like the Peace - finding it too HR trust training and just not for us. We only wanted to "touch" each other and our granddaughters. I do wear my heart on my arm and say what I'm thinking - often gets me in trouble; please realise I'm just thinking out loud. It helps me to bounce my ideas off FB.

March 11, 2017 at 8:54am
Love is stronger than death

"For you must realize," says Boehme, "that earth unfolds its properties and powers in union with Heaven aloft above us, and there is one Heart, one Being, one Will, one God, all in all." .... I believe we touched the hem of this one Heart. When all the scenarios, visions, cosmic purposes, and human posts fade to the stillness of hush, there is only love itself that sounds forth, the music that moves the stars and the sun. Finally, you stop running - from or toward - and simply open your heart, and that other intensity swallows you in its embrace. And for the duration of that embrace, whether it lasts a microsecond or the rest of your life, you peer into depth and see, with the utter certainty of your whole being, that it is the body of Christ - and that in it, all things do hold together. Cynthia Bourgeault "LOVE is stronger than DEATH." --- --- Pat, I love you forever; Love IS stronger than Death! I feel your presence in my soul.

March 11, 2017 at 9:50am
Lilacs

.

Pat loved lilacs and the Royal Botanical Gardens' Lilac Groves. Must remember when lilacs become available at St. Jacob's Market to buy a bunch to put on our grave. They were her favourite flower and favourite scent. I'm sure she is waiting for me to bring her some. Love you forever Patricia!

March 12, 2017 at 8:53am ·
Lack of privacy

Don't get me wrong but there are some disadvantages to having Pat's presence in my soul. Oh, there is the pleasure of her presence and the comfort it brings. But, I find myself purposely trying not to do anything that would displease her. Not that I would anyway because we were so much alike in morals, preferences, beliefs, and likes and dislikes. Being united spiritually into one entity by marriage and then death takes away your privacy - you are no longer alone. Oh, I know for a Christian, Christ is always with us but that is different, Pat when a physical entity, needed occasionally to be alone and so did I. How do you communicate? Feeling her and her emotional state (pleasure and displeasure, love) is not the same as being able to physically touch her and/or actually have a conversation in actual words. Oh well, God willing, I'll learn how to communicate as I did when the strokes took away her words; and when the time comes I'll be joining her in our place in Heaven. In the meantime, it's all one-sided conversations and spiritual touching. No, I'm not going mad and no this is not GRIEF speaking. Love IS stronger than Death and God willing, can grow stronger still after death.

March 12, 2017 at 4:17pm
Missing her physical company
.

Now who am I going to go for walks with along the river in Elora or along the river by the Boat House Tearoom in Guelph? Two of our favourite places to walk spring, summer and fall? Love you Pat forever!

March 12, 2017 at 4:53pm
Lonely

Hey I'm bored. Not feeling bad just deep down inside kind of lonely. Too cold to go out for a walk and no football on TV. Bruce MacNeil your photo of Elora has done that; I am remembering Pat and I walking along the mill run in downtown Elora, going in St. John's Church for a short prayer and going to a lovely tea house downtown just before her birthday in July. Oh, Pat I'll love you forever and will always remember lovely moments like this. The Good memories - and they far outnumber the bad - make life worthwhile. We have a lovely marriage, don't we? Yes "have", you in Heaven and me here, are still married and together in spirit. Know thyself and thou shalt know God.

March 13, 2017
A poem by Kumaris

"A precious point of conscious, blissful, light energy, the soul...
This is you
Imagine a tiny point located where thoughts come from.
That point thinks, remembers and decides.
This point is you.
The point where every emotion is born...
This is you.
A spiritual being interacting through the body...
This is you."   — Brahma Kumaris

This is the you that allows your loved ones to identify you after you die and begin your journey in Heaven. It is why the Apostles were able to recognize Jesus when he appeared to them in his resurrection body. It is the home of your soul – it is your soul!

Marriage make two souls one; as Pat's poem, "The world is Round," says:

"…we two are one:
Our story will be endless,
like the journey of the sun."

Our marriage – our one soul in two bodies – grew ever stronger as our love got further into our earthly journey. As Pat's "12th Anniversary Poem" said we grew evermore intertwined…
"yet beneath the grass and stone
intertwined their roots have grown'
so intimately webbed together,
neither one can tell his own.
So, with us: which flatly proves
futility of arguments
On which is which, and whose is whose."

When we are told to "know thyself" or" gnothi seauton" we are being told to know and commune with our Soul. Plato equated gnothi seauton with wisdom itself. Pat certainly knew herself and me intimately. We are taught, and I believe, the body is God's house; in knowing yourself you know God. For Pat, one journey is over and another has begun. She is with Christ in Heaven and with me here on earth. So, I am touching Christ through her.

What does it mean to be truly in love? In a nutshell, our quiet, sharing love was a spiritual union of souls: two individuals united before God but still separate, different individuals. It is still two individuals united as one but now Pat is truly with God preparing a place for me in Heaven. Pat has a celestial body in Heaven; I have not yet left my earthly body. Already I can, through a glass dimly, see what Pat is seeing in Heaven but only what she allows me to see. Love is giving each other the freedom to do their own thing and giving them time alone to know themselves. She is doing that now from heaven and I am trying not to call upon her for her comfort and peace, too much in my sorrow.

March 14, 2017 at 8:16am ·
God necessary for communion with Pat

"The words were gone; I had nothing to offer but myself. The silence revealed me to myself and held me before God. I was the expression of my prayer, and God was the response." This is what I mean when I say meditation allows me to communicate with Patricia and God
This One Holy Trinity is our true and eternal home.

March 15, 2017
The Trinity of marriage

I have mentioned before that when I awake from a nap I can often see Pat typing messages to me on something that looks like Facebook. It usually goes by fast and I have trouble reading it. This time it was different. I was waking up at 3 pm – the number three is important. Pat was complementing me on *Quiet Love ... eyes to see and words to tell the truths that are most true*. She typed that our marriage and love was like a community of three. At the centre of us was an eternal divine community of perfect love. The Bible says that God is love, but the only way God can be love is for God to be a community of divine persons. Love does not exist in a monad. God is that eternal community of love and so was our marriage. Each person of the Trinity is irreducibly and uniquely itself, distinct in three persons, and yet is perfectly united in being, love, and purpose. It is a true community of perfect love. It is like what I drew as the circles that took James in on page 93 of Quiet Love

In John's gospel, before his death Jesus prays to his Father, "23 I in them, and thou in me, that they may be made perfect in one; and that the world may know that thou hast sent me, and hast loved them, as thou hast loved me." John 17:23 King James Version (KJV)

Jesus makes the astounding claim that the triune God's ultimate purpose is to include us in this eternal trinitarian dance of love. The Father sends the Son to be one of us. By faith and baptism, we are included in his relationship with the Father. By the gift of the Holy Spirit, we cry, "Abba, Father!" We are in the Son, and the Son is in the Father, and we come to share in this eternal community of love through the Holy Spirit.

St. Augustine, also confirms this: "Now when I, who am asking about this, love anything, there are three things present: I myself, what I love, and love itself. For I cannot love love unless I love a lover; for there is no love where nothing is loved. So, there are three things: the lover, the loved and the love."

Her waking me up to this truth is proof to me that we never separated and Pat and I are one soul. Pat is indeed in heaven preparing a place for us. We are well on our way to becoming GOD and us.

March 15 at 5:33pm
Hole within

You know that hole within me? It is a perfect fit for Pat so nobody else can fit or fill it. It will remain an empty hole until I join Pat in our place in Heaven. I wouldn't have it any other way. Pat, I love you forever.

March 16, 2017 at 8:44am
God and us

I woke this morning feeling incredibly lonely and it was almost painful. Oh, I expect to be sad, but the feeling of loneliness has its own and subtly different kind of pain. I love Pat so much and she loves me so much and now she is in heaven and physically gone. It is an awful feeling. I yearn for the physical her. I want her back. I miss her. I need her. I need to talk to her about mundane things like what she wants for dinner or what needs done around the house or other mundane things. And she is not there. She is not there physically. I am lonely for the physical Pat. I thought I was going to go first - usually the husband dies first. Interestingly in this void of loneliness is when I feel most in contact with the spiritual Pat. After one knows somebody for 48 years, they can typically tell when they are close. This is true for Pat's spirit as well - I'm aware of the presence of the spiritual Pat inside me and near me. I talk to her but she answers in feelings. I feel her love and peace. The thing is I'm not at peace. She has "... the peace of God, which passeth all understanding." I don't yet. Sometimes our peace crumbles because we've placed our trust in our loved one, our spouse, always being there for us instead of completely in God. Okay I'm guilt for not putting my complete trust in God and instead depending on Pat always being there - definitely a case of us and

81

GOD. I must begin to trust God more so that we, both Pat and I, can build a strong trust relationship with God that will restore my peace. I have to start on the journey to GOD and us! Oh, God I believe, help me in my unbelief. Pat, I love you forever! Amen.

March 16 at 9:23pm ·
At Tai Chi

Interesting experience at Tai Chi this morning. When it came to an actual set, I started in a meditative frame of mind - actually my mind was almost empty. That's when I felt Pat taking over my movements. Best darned set I ever did - Pat was better at the moves than I when alive and she continues to be better than I after death even when in my body. I was so moved that I had to sneak out, go upstairs to the Church and kneel at the communion rail to keep the feeling of Pat being in control for just a bit longer. Pat, I'll love you forever. Thank you!

March 17, 2017 at 9:38am
An old loneliness

Seems to me I was better at being alone way back before I met Pat. I do still need occasional time alone but this is far too much. The house seems so empty without Pat. Despite this, I would have it no other way. I do not want the void within me to go; it constantly reminds me she is still with me spiritually. I wonder if that void is actually Pat or maybe the connection to our place in heaven. Patricia, I love you and I miss you terribly!

March 17, 2017 at 12:08pm
Miss her still

.

Odd the things you miss a loved one doing at her desk next to you. I actually miss Pat sitting at her desk glued quietly to her computer playing Angband for hours. Angband is a freeware, open-source computer game of dungeon exploration, based very loosely on the works of J.R.R. Tolkien.

March 17 at 6:25pm ·
Her dream
Patricia Bow had a dream. Pat wrote: " Writing a book is an achievement, if it's a half way decent work. But not publishing somehow leaves it unfinished." and her dream was " everything I wrote would be published, distributed, reviewed, and read." Well I think now I have filled her dream with Quiet Love the memoir and the Poems. The only thing she started writing I haven't published is her planned 4th book in the Mythrin series, Festival of Dragons. She was writing it for Granddaughter Nora. There are only 20 chapters done but the chapter outline, FOD chaps & timeline, FOD Character, and the notes for the rest of it are fairly complete. Nobody I know writes in

the same style. It will just have to remain unfinished and unpublished. I'll keep it though (files, notes, maps and all); maybe one of her granddaughters will one day finish it for her.

March 18 at 5:43am ·
Psalm

Patricia Bow's favourite Psalm is featured on Forward Day by Day today. Her desire for the Nova Scotia trip was just not what the Good Shepherd wanted for her. I'm sure Pat is where Christ wanted her to be - in green pastures, beside still waters, you don't always get what you ask for; Christ did spare her the pain and gave her a peaceful death. We, Pat and I, are thankful for that. Mind you there still are tears.

March 18 at 11:52am ·
Pattern?

Pat died on the day after the Feast of the Epiphany (the 12th day of Christmas), so on the first day of Epiphany. Epiphany reveals Jesus as the Divine Son and Savior sent by God the Father to atone for the sins of mankind. It is a time of healing and fellowship so; the first day of Epiphany is a good day to die if any day is. It is a sign of Christ's love and mercy and that she went straight to heaven.

"O God, who wonderfully created the dignity of human nature and still more wonderfully restored it, grant, we pray, that we may share in the divinity of Christ, who humbled himself to share in our humanity."

The Epiphany season is full of manifestations the six Sundays which follow Epiphany are known as the time of manifestation. I am looking forward to Pat and I growing every more together through these "manifestations" and seeing Pat and feeling her presence every more strongly.

Pat, I love you forever! LOVE IS Stronger than Death.

March 18 at 12:08pm
Manifestations·

After Pat's "manifestations" during Epiphany I am expecting this Easter Sunday to be something really special. I expect some sort of revelation about our place in heaven and about joining Pat in heaven to spend all eternity with God. But if it doesn't come I won't be unhappy because it will come in time.

March 18 at 5:18pm ·
I'm okay

Hey, I'm more okay than my friends and family think I am. I believe and both Pat and Christ are comforting me. I cannot understand how those with little or no faith can bear a Grief like this. It is my faith, my Church and my Priest that are getting me through this. Pat went first

85

because she was closer to God and I still had a bit of a way to go. She is helping me greatly and preparing a place for us in Heaven. Hey, it is perfectly natural for one spouse to want to join the other on the great journey in heaven. Look suicide is out of the question. There are absolutely no grounds for believing that death by that route would reunite me with her. Why should it? I might be digging an eternally unbridgeable chasm. Disobedience is not the way to get nearer to the obedient. This thought brings absolute terror to my spirit. It is the prospect of seeing Pat again, being a united soul again and attaining heaven with her that keeps me going. Look we are still the one soul our marriage made us - her in heaven me here. We both are spiritual introverts. Joining groups never was our thing. It is also okay to pray for death to come soon as Simeon did and as even Christ did. Also, if you are mortally ill it is okay to make use of doctor assisted death. But I am not mortally ill. Please stop telling me to get grief consoling. I am being looked after by God, Pat, my nearest and dearest especially my son James Bow, my Priest and by those in my Church. The free counselling session I just watched on FB filled me with dread and horror. It is definitely NOT for me. Eric Bow

March 19 at 7:10pm ·
Snatched kiss

Looked out the window to see a married couple walking two dogs - one each. The dogs made them stop and face each out. The couple (early 30s I'd say) took the opportunity to kiss unaware that someone was watching. It is the kind of thing Pat and I used to do a lot - steal a kiss on the occasion of a beautiful sunset. Made me happy but also a bit sad because it wasn't Pat and I. Pat, I love you forever.

March 19 at 7:46pm ·
Photos do help

"Look at Photographs of Your Loved One — It's healthy to keep photographs around you and look at them regularly. One widower I know keeps a picture of his dear one beside his bed. Every night before he goes to sleep, he blows her a kiss. He likes knowing that she's still beside him. Although his friends told him to remove photographs in his house, he said to me, "Why would I want to erase all those wonderful memories?"

Not only do I have photos of Pat in every room my Windows 10 background and screensavers are also pictures of Pat. Beautiful good memories I want to remember forever. This picture idea is very good advice - pictures make you feel better so why not?

March 20, 2017
ACQUAINTED WITH GRIEF

There is a question that keeps coming up on all the Grief boards I read: "does my loved one in heaven feel grief and sorrow for her earthly losses?" There doesn't seem to be a satisfactory answer; especially as Christ, in Isaiah 52:3, is described as: "A man of sorrows, and acquainted with grief." The question is important to me as well. It has been very comforting to me to believe I spared Pat the pain I felt and still feel occasionally, by not departing first (as if I had any choice).

Pat obviously felt the pain when she learned she was dying. She wrote on Wednesday November 16, 2016:

I hate the fact that I am making several loved people unhappy.

The other thing I hate is the prospect of pain. I am terrified. I am a complete coward when it comes to pain. I am told things can be done to control pain, but I'm not sure I believe it.

So much I will lose. The beauty of the Earth; of the skies, of colours. I see it all turning and turning to darkness.

So much loss, such pain.

Please God, please, please, please.

March 20, 2017
Did Pat carry this into heaven?

When did this feeling of loss, pain and sorrow go away for both Christ and Pat; was it immediately upon leaving the earthly body or does it stay, since Pat being one with me feels what I am feeling and we believe Christ to understand pain and sorrow?

There are three places in the Bible where it is promised God will wipe away the tears. Isaiah 25:8 (KJV) "He will swallow up death in victory; and the Lord God will wipe away tears from off all faces; and the rebuke of his people shall he take away from off all the earth: for the Lord hath spoken it."; Revelation 7:17 (KJV) "For the Lamb which is in the midst of the throne shall feed them, and shall lead them unto living fountains of waters: and God shall wipe away all tears from their eyes." and Revelation 21:4 (KJV) "And God shall wipe away all tears from their eyes; and there shall be no more death, neither sorrow, nor crying, neither shall there be any more pain: for the former things are passed away."

The question becomes when does this happen and for Pat does it wipe away only her own pain and not the pain she feels from being one with me? I don't have an answer, but, I feel Pat is at PEACE now and we remain one! Both Christ and Pat are comforting me.

3 Blessed be God, even the Father of our Lord Jesus Christ, the Father of mercies, and the God of all comfort; 4 Who comforteth us in all our tribulation, that we may be able to comfort them which are in any trouble, by the comfort wherewith we ourselves are comforted of God. 5 For as the sufferings of Christ abound in us, so our

consolation also aboundeth by Christ. 2 Corinthians 1:3-5 (KJV)

March 20 at 10:16pm ·
True love poems

Pat's poems reach right into my (our) soul - especially 'Basic' and '12th Anniversary Poem'. Our souls did become one like the two trees..."... beneath the grass and stone intertwined their roots have grown, / so intimately webbed together neither one can tell his own. / So, with us: which flatly proves / Futility of arguments / On which is which, and whose is whose." So please remember what we say during the wedding ceremony "Wherefore they are no more twain, but one flesh. What therefore God hath joined together, let not man put asunder." We are entwined forever - me on earth she in heaven. Love is stronger than death. I love her little more than I love life itself. Neither of us want to be "freed." I want that hole in my heart to last till Pat and I meet again in heaven and God heals us. I don't want to return to "normal." I want to feel Pat's presence within and beside me as long as I live. I'll love Pat forever. That is what it is meant to be.

March 21st at 6:42am
Communicating ·

It seems Pat communicates with me when I need it most. This morning, I was almost awake when I saw Pat and I, in a sort of room she was typing on what again looked like a computer screen with Facebook, and I was watching over her shoulder. It was a lot clearer than the other times but still required squinting at the dot-matrix picture. Surprisingly this time, it was almost sexual. We were there touching, she in a radiant in-between form and me in my present form. It felt sexual and very pleasant. Pat was the one who brought up the sexuality of this communion. She typed that it was okay to feel this. She typed or maybe said in my mind that this type of communication creates the new "body" we need for our second journey together. I, at this moment, knew LOVE remains and creates the united eternal body through our communion. I found myself yearning for that final consummation when my earthly body, also has been left behind and we are reunited in our resurrection body. Maybe God will answer my prayer and take me soon BUT it will not seem long at least for her, if he doesn't or for me either if I have more communions with Pat like this morning's. It keeps me moving forward toward Pat - striving toward that fullness of being, God and Us, that can never be had alone. I understand as never before: LOVE is stronger than DEATH - it is what is promised in our marriage ceremony, a mystical union made by God of two souls. Pat, I shall love you forever!

March 21st at 10:49am ·

Pat watching me

Pat seems to be following me on Facebook - though my eyes I guess. Okay Pat what now? I've been trying to complete the things you wanted to do (your bucket list) where I could by myself or by asking someone else to complete it for you when I don't have the skill. (I know you would want me to offer compensation and I will when they complete it. I have run out of projects. Please give me some sign of what you want done next taking into consideration my skill level and that you were and are a one of a kind person and very talented. Love you forever!

March 22, 2017 ·
Single thought

Odd how a single thought - Ms. Owl missing her grandma Pat - can send you back into tears. I miss the earthly Pat so much and I have the comfort of the eternal Pat. I can imagine what my granddaughters without the touch of the eternal Pat is feeling - all the emptiness and tears. It hurts me too.

March 23, 2017
Am I dying

I woke up this morning thinking I am dying; odd as physically I feel fine. No aches and pains or lumps in the legs or migraines like Pat. While I am eagerly and impatiently waiting to see Pat again, I have no intention of joining her by my own hand. Look suicide is out of the question. There are absolutely no grounds for believing that death by that route would reunite me with her. Why should it? By suicide, I might be digging an eternally unbridgeable chasm between me and her. Disobedience is not the way to get nearer to the obedient. This thought, that I could lose her forever, brings absolute terror to my spirit. Besides there is no painless, absolutely sure, way to kill oneself. The prospect of trying, not succeeding and spending my last days an immobile invalid also terrorises me.

Part of this feeling that I am dying comes from Pat's three predictions of our death before 2020 in her dairies for the years 2000, 2010 and 2014. She was absolutely accurate in predicting her own death even if the diagnosis on the anniversary of our first date came as a surprise and great shock. She never thought of her six siblings, she would be the first to die. She also thought the Smiths died from heart problems or strokes not cancer. Well the pancreatic cancer caused blood clots, which in turn caused the strokes which killed her.

The biggest cause of my premonition that I am dying comes from a pattern I see forming. Her diagnosis on the anniversary of our first date parallels the beginning of our earthly journey together; that diagnosis was the beginning of our heavenly journey united though I'm here on earth and she is in heaven. The palliative care period is like our intense dating up to when she went home for the Christmas holiday, only this time she went home to God. Then there is the loving moment of my feeling her kiss me the day after she died, like when she came back from Ottawa after New Year 1969. On my birthday in 1969, we were together; this year I felt her with me and discovered this on her computer: "Death is not extinguishing the light; it is only putting out the lamp because the dawn has come." — Rabindranath Tagore   Then around the anniversary of our engagement this year, February 14th, I felt "Something has changed! I am now aware of my wife, Patricia's presence touching me. Started last night and grew stronger at Mass that morning. She was there with me, her presence and her spiritual strength comforting and supporting me. That is the thing: - in 1969 June 21, we were married and began our marriage. It these events are indeed paralleling 1968/69 doesn't this mean I join Pat in heaven on June 21, 2017?

Wait there is more, Pat began Advent by being the fifth reader at Holy Saviour's Advent Lessons and Carols service on the first Sunday of Advent. Pat died on the day after the Feast of the Epiphany (the 12th day of Christmas), so on the first day of Epiphany. I am expecting this Easter Sunday to be something really special. I expect some sort of revelation about our place in heaven and about joining Pat in heaven to spend all eternity with God. But if it doesn't come I won't be unhappy because it will come in time. I'll die when it is my time to die.

Thursday March 23 at 6:30
Roots

Pat and I were married for almost 48 years - that is more than twice as long as she lived with her family in Ottawa. more than enough years for our roots to grow together.... "beneath the grass and stone / intertwined their roots have grown, / so intimately webbed together, / neither one can tell his own." You know in nature those roots remain together for centuries. So too us, we are one for all eternity neither knowing "which is which and whose is whose" in the loving arms of Christ.

Friday March 24 at 9:20 am
Paradise now

Some of you may know that first Christmas (1968) I gave Pat a book of Cohen's poems, a loaf of bread, a bottle of wine all under boughs cut from Christmas trees as per: "A BOOK of Verses underneath the Bough, / A Jug of Wine, a Loaf of Bread—and Thou / Beside me singing in the Wilderness—/ O, Wilderness were Paradise enow!"

This past Christmas was this: "Ah, make the most of what we yet may spend, / Before we too into the Dust descend; / Dust unto Dust, and under Dust to lie, / Sans Wine, sans Song, sans Singer, and—sans End!"

and now:

"Ah, with the Grape my fading Life provide,
And wash my Body whence the Life has died,
And lay me, shrouded in the living Leaf,
By some not unfrequented Garden-side....

Yon rising Moon that looks for us again—
How oft hereafter will she wax and wane;
How oft hereafter rising look for us
Through this same Garden—and for one in vain!

And when like her O Sákí, you shall pass
Among the Guests star-scatter'd on the Grass,
And in your joyous errand reach the spot
Where I made One—turn down an empty Glass!

.... From Omar Khayyám

Poets really do see clearly through the glass! They touch
our very souls.

Friday March 24, 2017 at 3:50 pm
Poetry stopped

I wondered in *Quiet Love* why Pat stopped writing poetry
after 1985. Just realized what could be a reason: in 1986
Pat turned 40! Remember we were hippies and used to
preach not to trust anyone over 40. Well 40 is the

beginning of middle age and many women go into a deep depression upon turning 40. She began to wonder if she had wasted her life. Why didn't she have a book published? What have I done with the first half of my life? Was she really mid-life or would she die sooner than the average life expectancy?

Researchers from Dartmouth College in Hanover, N.H., and the University of Warwick in Coventry, England, after scouring 35 years' worth of data on two million people from 80 nations, have concluded that there is, indeed, a consistent pattern in depression and happiness levels that is age-related and leaves us most blue during midlife. They found a similar pattern in 70 other countries and in North America 40 is the beginning of mid life for women.

It was also probably an motherhood thing as well: James entered his teens in 1985 and wasn't having an easy time emotionally. Pat worried about him all his life and more so in his teens and right up to his marrying Erin.

In determining to do something about accomplishing her dream of publishing a novel in English, she made a bad choice in 1986. She joined the Romance Writers of America and got a Romance Writer Agent. She was in the wrong genre for her and had numerous failures trying to write a romance novel. That added to her depression.

I think all this also explains why she got increasingly depressed introverted and unhappy after 1986. She did however turn this depression and lack of confidence once she retired. She was finally able to spend her days the way she wanted.

Saturday March 25, 2017
Bucket List

Not everyone has a "bucket list" I don't. There are no places I want to travel to; in fact, I hate travel. However, I so wanted Pat to have her wish to return to White Point Beach for our 48th anniversary this June. We had booked it and the round trip on the Ocean train. She prayed for both of us to remain healthy until after this trip. Sometimes God says NO! At such times, it is very difficult to say, "Thine will be done" Amen

"Not that I am (I think) in much danger of ceasing to believe in God. The real danger is of coming to believe such dreadful things about Him. The conclusion I dread is not 'So there's no God after all,' but 'So this is what God's really like. Deceive yourself no longer.''

March 25, 2017 11 am
Grief keeps returning

It's one of those bad days. Pat was absolutely right when she wrote on November 16th, "To Eric it was a terrible blow. Maybe he'll never recover either." She knows me better than I know myself. I will probably never recover until I join her in heaven. You'd think it would be enough to feel her presence and her comforting me and her Peace that passeth all understanding. It isn't though - I want and need more.

"For in grief nothing "stays put." One keeps on emerging from a phase, but it always recurs. Round and round. Everything repeats. Am I going in circles, or dare I hope I am on a spiral?

But if a spiral, am I going up or down it?

How often -- will it be for always? -- how often will the vast emptiness astonish me like a complete novelty and make me say, "I never realized my loss till this moment"? The same leg is cut off time after time." — C.S. Lewis, A Grief Observed.

Saturday March 25, 2017 at 4:15pm
C. S. Lewis seems to speak directly to me in Pat's own words.

Wow this is remarkable! In "Quiet Love" I quote Pat's thoughts on our marriage as "sort of communicating bubbles" and how she thought our type of marriage, two touching circles, "is the best". Reading C. S. Lewis "A Grief Observed" I discover this passage: "Suppose that the earthly lives she and I shared for a few years are in reality only the basis for, or prelude to, or earthly appearance of, two unimaginable, super-cosmic, eternal somethings. Those somethings could be pictured as spheres or globes. Where the plane of Nature cuts through them – that is, in earthly life – they appear as two circles (circles are slices of spheres). Two circles that touched. But those two circles, above all the point at which they touched, are the very thing I am mourning for, homesick for, famished for. You tell me 'she goes on'. But my heart and body are crying out, come back, come back. Be a circle, touching my circle on the plane of Nature.

I want to assure Lewis, though I expect he already knows, that the one point where those two eternal spheres touch as earthly circles became one in marriage and continue to touch forever. That is why we still feels our spouses' presence after she is gone. I want to shout out to him, NO all that is not gone; the former things have NOT passed away. Love is stronger than Death. It is not about 'family reunions on the further shore'. Yes, we know it couldn't be like that. We do see our loved ones again; this sure belief rests on two pillars of Christian belief. One is the blessed hope that we will see Jesus again (Titus 2:13). The other is the assurance that our present bodies will be raised from the dead, immortal (1 Cor. 15:12-57). Together, these pillars provide a basis for believing we will recognize our loved ones in heaven. After all, if we can recognize the Lord Jesus, possessing the perfectly restored and glorified bodies to do so, it follows that we will recognize other believers, including our loved ones. Pat wrote: "Eric had his own brainstorm recently, also concerned with freedom of the will. His view is that we are like ships on the ocean. We can't control the external circumstances of our lives – the currents, the storms, the calms and winds. But we can make use of our sails and rudders to control the way we meet these circumstances, and we can plot our course as well as possible." C. S. Lewis uses the same metaphor of our lives being ships on a sea. He describes marriage as one ship. "One flesh. Or, if you prefer, one ship. The starboard engine has gone. I, the port engine, must chug along somehow till we make harbour. Or rather, till the journey ends. How can I assume a harbour? A lee shore, more likely, a black night, a deafening gale, breakers ahead – and any lights shown from land probably being waved by wreckers. Such was H's landfall. Such was my mother's. I say their landfalls; not their arrivals."

C. S. Lewis is the most influential apologist for the Anglican church of the twentieth century. It is very comforting to find Pat and I have used the same words and ideas as him. It shows we may just be on the right track in our journey to God and us.

Sunday March 26, 2017 at 3:22 pm
Bad Dream

I had a dream last night about Pat trying to escape me in an old Volkswagen camper van (yes, a Hippie camper) parked in front of our house. I brought her back into the house and threatened to tell the authorities she was breaking her vows. There are many implications in this dream. But the one that really has filled me with fear is Pat wants to escape from me; she doesn't want to be in my presence comforting me. As she wrote in her dairies she wants to be alone - she needed to be alone at times then. But she is in Heaven now in the arms of Christ; she can't be completely alone ever again. I am afraid, there is the fluttering in the stomach, the restlessness, the yawning. I keep on swallowing. Yes, I am terrified! We both at our marriage agreed with "Wherefore they are no more twain, but one flesh. What therefore God hath joined together, let not man put asunder." Oh, Pat I still love you and will love you better after death. This dream has really got me shaken. Please Pat do not leave me alone.

Monday March 27, 2017
Sharing the Grief Journey

Another insight into Patricia and why we were so well matched. Being an only child and being the middle child of seven results in our sharing a lot of characteristics. It is also why I'm having trouble coping with being alone. Pat and I actually cultivated being alone – going to gatherings was out of character for us. Pat was introverted and I was always a loner. We both were very satisfied with our own company and each other's company. Don't get Pat wrong, she loved her siblings but did not need to be in their

102

company very much. She was content to know that her immediate family members were all within reach somewhere, linked to her by genetic threads. In fact, she was not just introverted, in her own words, she was "also reserved/private, and shy – three different things. The triple whammy. But I'm not a misanthrope, or not yet." Okay it is not helping me now that those closest to me are even smaller than was Pat's circle. But unlike Pat, I don't think it a sin to dislike gatherings and groups.

Pat wrote: "…I suspect I am simply not that interested in real people (as opposed to fictional ones) although I have the greatest good will towards them. This is probably something close to a sin. I also see it in church, where Eric likes forming social connections, while I would rather just go there to worship."

Again, Pat knows me better than I know myself. She's right I enjoy the people at Church but after the service not the chatting before the service nor the Peace during the service. Now I find comfort from those I have gotten to know at Holy Saviour Waterloo as well as from the BCP services.

It is probably a good thing Pat died before me. Though she was the stronger, she would have had a harder time with grief than me. Her fear of pain – believe me grief is PAIN – her hate of networking and her introversion would be a problem for her grief journey. She was just too private. Unfortunately for her the grief journey needs her

103

to reach out to family and friends and to truly communicate with them.

I am so glad Pat shared her family with me and they welcomed me into the family. They are a big help now – especial Deanna who like me has lost a spouse. She is helping a lot with my grief journey. And Pat herself being near me, in my soul, communing with me and sharing the Peace that passes all understanding that comes from being in the arms of Christ are a big help. Pat, I love you forever.

March 29, 2017 by thebows99krug

True Love is for all eternity

I am reading Vanauken's "Under the Mercy" and am deeply moved and completely agree with his thoughts on marriage (the one-flesh union) which LOVE promises and points to. Marriage vows are NOT vows to each other but the vows are THEIR promise to God as well as each other. The vows are a gift from one to the other; not a protestation of love as those who write their own vows don't seem to understand. Here and now they are saying, each to the other: "This is my promise, my vow before God. This you can trust. This you can lean on in the bad times for all eternity, whatever I may feel at any given moment, I WILL be faithful. Never fear. You have my word made before God. Pat and I were never out of LOVE with each other. We wanted nothing so much as the good of the other. Our Quiet Love was cherishing, wanting each other's best good and shall last for all eternity. Yes, the one-flesh union endures and grows in Heaven. I clearly saw in Pat's writings that she believed and felt as I do that our quiet love kept getting stronger and was a foretaste of Heaven. A person alone is incomplete. The mystical union by marriage into one is the true second birth, a fusion of their personalities into the beginning of the eternal Resurrection body that happens after death. When the body dies, the soul is taken up into divine Love and illuminated with God's light to await its other half. – our love keeps right on growing. It belongs to "the conscious circle of spiritual life we Christians call the communion of Saints. It is what I am feeling when I feel Pat's presence in and near me. Pat, I truly love you forever!

Friday March 31, 2017

The Presence is REAL

Pat is at peace, that same love and peace of God also surrounds and uphold all of us, her family, and all who mourn. Neither death nor any created thing is able to separate us from the divine love we share in a Holy Communion that continues beyond death. Now we see through a glass dimly, but then we shall see clearly face to face. I compare the mystery of death to the mystery and wonder of life itself. Once, we were within the security of the womb and faced the trauma of birth not knowing the awesome wonders nor the love that awaited us in dimensions yet to be experienced. So, shall it be in death. 'Death is not the extinguishing of the light. It is but the putting out of the lamp, for the dawn has come.' — Rabindranath Tagore

The relationship between a husband and wife is different from all other family relationships. In no other case does God join two into one. When you lose a spouse you really do lose half of yourself and a big hole is left inside you. Now Pat died soon after reaching three score and 10; I am strong so am expected to reach four score. That thought fills me with horror; I really don't want to live 6 more years without my other half. But Lord, Thine will not mine.

Something has changed! I am now aware of my wife, Patricia's presence touching me every day. It is as if Pat and I were made whole again; Oh, I still miss her physical presence and her words and tears still come at small memories. But she is there with me, her presence and her spiritual strength comfort and support me. Surely, we shall dwell united in the house of the Lord forever.

Okay how do I know this is not a trick of the mind. I recently read this: "This feeling has been called "The sensed Presence." The brain scientist's explanation for this lies in the idea that we have two senses of self, one on each side of the brain. Ordinarily, we rely primarily on the one on the left, where language, both inner and outer, is produced. When a person is having the sensed presence, the senses of self on the two sides of the brain have fallen out of phase with each other. The right-sided self comes out where the left-sided self can experience it. It's being projected, or its a projected being. It's real if you are." Sounds plausible.

The thing is I'm not convinced. Feeling Pat's presence is like all the times we felt each other in the house and knew we were not alone. I'd wake from a nap and just feel Pat's absence because she had gone out for a walk alone. As Pat said, you feel the other's presence because he/she affects the vibrations and atmosphere of the whole house. Each of us have a presence that can't be explained by the "brain scientists". Why is it a response to grief when your spouse dies and not when we were both happily alive? We are more than the sum total of our physical parts. There is something in all of us that is there watching, in command as the brain and body does it's thing. It surely is the soul. I am sure when God designed us to be like Him it was not the physical body that resulted. It has to be the soul. I have read that medical studies have found a miniscule loss of weight when one dies. It has to be the soul leaving the body, taken up in the arms of Christ. How is it I am able to feel Pat's presence? I think I feel Pat's presence – I feel her thinking, her pleasure and displeasure at a thought or emotion almost as I feel my own. I am feeling her emotions and not mine as they can be quite different – she's at peace now while I'm still on the grief journey. I also think I feel her love for me almost as strongly as I feel my own love for her. But this is no different than before she died; we were always able to feel each other's love. To love you need someone to love – love is always directed. I seem to know when she is pleased or displeased. This is different as when alive we show what we are feeling in physical signs that are very difficult to conceal; now I feel her emotions inside me. One odd think about her presence in me is I seem to be able to see (okay with my eyes partly closed or completely closed) what she is seeing – mostly the words she is typing or writing. All I can say about that is Pat was a word person and I miss her words very deeply. Thank God for her dairies, poems and writings. I definitely felt her kiss me the day after she died – what sense in me was that?

So, I do believe in the real presence. We are not two separate souls separated by death but a continuous united soul in the eternal body. Our love allows us to share her new eternal body in the LOVE of Christ. I must not allow myself to slip into despair because it is OUR life I am affecting. Pat and I put our love first. We did everything together. After all we were and are still one flesh. We shared and wanted to be together. We wanted the Good for each other. I believe Pat and I found in each other our true Soul Mate our hard to find one True Love. In Pat's words: "For you and I are so entwined / that we can read each other's mine / at times, a simple exercise."

April

INVOCATION
1962.
Titled April 6/92.

Tonight, the sky is less than pure
and winds that fly across the towers
stumble on stone, hard shod, unsure.
The darkness drowns the quiet flowers

that glow less scarlet than before
I gave my heart and mind free rein
to gallop over valley and shore
and call up shadows of lasting pain.

Small spirits I cannot rebind
rise up to haunt me, and I find
the devils that prompt me unawares
are those I wakened by my prayers.

Sunday April 2, 2017 at 8 am
Too much on Pat

There are some who tell me I am posting and thinking of
Pat far too much and it shows I need help or at least anti
depressants. Hey when she was alive she was always on
my mind and nearby. We often shared our thoughts good
and bad. When you are down it is good to talk with your
loved one - we are after all ONE and want only good for
the other half. I need to continue to talk to Pat and
develop my ideas, especially my ideas on life after death
and the Resurrection body and love being forever. She no
longer has words but she is with me and I feel her
thoughts and sometimes see her typing an answer on that
screen that looks like a Facebook screen. I and she both
got depressed when she was alive - why am I not allowed
after her death? We all deal with grief in our own way;
there is no right time for one to "get over it". Besides it is
who I am and I expect to carry that Pat sized hole in my
being until we are reunited in Heaven and she fills it and
we are whole again. Pat, I love you forever. Thoughts of
her continue to provide comfort and our love continues to
grow stronger.

Sunday April 2, 2017 at 5:20
Life after death / marriage as a Trinity

Pat wrote, "Perhaps it is enough simply to believe the spirit does not died." We all have some doubts about life after death. I can't imagine that there isn't life after death but there is still that little nagging occasional doubt that Pat had when she wrote that sentence. The little essence that was in Pat and is in me can't just snuff out at death. It is far too real. Yet there are some who believe this.

All Christians and Jews I talk to believe in life after death and look forward to rejoining their loved ones in heaven. Mind you many have not thought it though and have no idea what heaven or life is going to be like after death. I suspect but don't know that all world religions believe in life after death. A god and life after death are after all what "religion" is all about. Life after death is a compulsion of the human mind; it is very difficult for a human being not to believe in it even if it is just a belief that something lives on after we die.

Christians believe Christ's promise that there is a place for each of use believers prepared by Christ himself. Yes, Pat and I believe that completely. We also believe the New Testament passages promising we will recognize our loved ones even in their new eternal Christ-like body and that our loved ones will be waiting for us when we get to heaven to help our rebirth into the eternal resurrection body.

Pat and I also believed very strongly in the sacrament of marriage. We believe that in marriage two entities are made one by God never to be separated. Even by death itself. In fact, we are made whole again by death. We also both believe that love continues after death and continues to grow every stronger. As described by Pat, though we are two individuals we are still united as one when we depart this life here on earth. We are a trinity – Pat, I and the person that our love is. The third person, Love, is the binding force just like the Holy Ghost in the divine Trinity. Christians have always believed that God is Love and that LOVE is what unites us all in the communion of Saints.

"For you must realize," says Jacob Boehme, (Confessions) "that earth unfolds its properties and powers in union with Heaven aloft above us, and there is one Heart, one Being, one Will, one God, all in all." On the Grief Journey, you eventually stop running and simply look in your own heart and are swallowed by the embrace of your loved one in her eternal resurrection body (explains that kiss the day after she died) – you are united again in the love of Christ. You realize nothing has changed, you are whole again and nothing, no part of your love is taken away. As physically lonely as you are you continue to grow in love forever.

Love bears all things, believes all things, hopes all things, endures all things. Enduring is part of Christian love, the love which brought Pat and I together in marriage. The end of the great journey is when you discover God has been calling you to become true man and wife united in one eternal resurrection body in Heaven. C. S. Lewis' GOD and US at last. Christianity has always held that the difference is, in fact, soul deep, that the souls and resurrected bodies of men and women are masculine and feminine through all eternity. Men and women are equal but different. They complement each other. They are the Chinese Yin and Yang the founding principal of the universe.

Wednesday April 5, 2017
Entwined after death

It just occurred to me that Easter makes it possible for our departed loved ones to be present with us. If we are entwined in life we will be entwined after death. It is both marriage making us one and Christ defeating death. In Pat's words: "For you and I are so entwined / that we can read each other's mine / at times, a simple exercise." Hallelujah, He is risen indeed!

April 6, 2017 at 10:15
Happy Easter. He is risen!

The writings on grief are filled with survivors blaming God for their loss and as a result abandoning their faith. Some religions try to comfort the bereaved by saying it was God's will and there are some that say the deceased did something to deserve to die. All in the belief that because God knows what is going to happen He wills it to happen. Nothing could be further from the reality of God; God is outside time and sees what is in time all at once. Yes, he is all powerful and could spare the deceased death but, that would be to deny us our free will. God created the universe, probably in a big bang but, the universe follows logical laws not God's will. We are as subject to the laws of nature as any physical object. We die because that is how our bodies work or nature takes us in a perfect storm not because of the will of God. We should not be blaming either the deceased or God for the death. God didn't cause Pat's death, cancer did. What God did was take her up in His arms to the place in Heaven promised by Christ. Rather than ending, our love continues beyond the grave. This is the meaning of Easter. Patricia is in the arms of Christ. Hallelujah!

Thursday April 8, 2017 at 9 am
Real presence

Eventually C. S. Lewis accepted the presence of Joy, his departed wife, though he believed it was not the soul but her intellect. He speaks of the experience, "It was incredibly unemotional. Just the impression of her mind momentarily facing my own." He calls it more like intelligence and attention. To me that is what the soul is – intelligence and attention. It is that which watches us, that unites two in love into one. When I feel Pat's presence it is what I feel but I also feel the essence of Pat, her feelings, pleasure, love and peace.

I had such a feeling this morning as I was waking but still dreaming. I am sure it was Pat – it had her personal identity and true love. Pat was creating (drawing) an animated heart (beating) covered in rose wreaths and growing until it covered the entire field of vision. I felt her love and knew instantly that she was telling me she still loved me, that love is forever and our love is still growing. Yes, more than just intellect and attention but just as real as Lewis' Joy presence.

Such after death appearances refute the claims by some that the dead have "gone to their rest", that "their work is done", and that they "sleep in peace". While they are at peace and in the arms of Christ, their work is not done, they are not resting, and they are growing and preparing for the birth of two entities into that one resurrection body in heaven. There is soul work still to be done. As Rev. Cynthia Bourgeault (LOVE is stronger than DEATH) writes, "the very purpose of true love is to form a whole that is greater than the sum of its parts and, through the strength of that union, imperious to death."

Rev Cynthia also explains why often somehow these after death appearances feel sexual. She writes, "And there is also sexuality that, clarified of the craving and attachment, is truly Eucharistic – "This is my body, given for you" – A drawing near to the other with all that one has and is: in conscious love; to give the innermost gift of oneself, in the most intimate foretaste of divine union that can be known in human flesh."

Sunday April 9, 2017 at 9:20
Sharing.

When married couples no longer share their deepest feelings, thoughts, and experiences with one another it can leave them feeling disconnected and alone. After the death of a spouse you need not become lonely if your Love results in a real presence. That Real Presence can offer a truly deep connection. My answer to Erin's question about my annoying Pat in heaven a lot, is actually not a joke. It is because of our deep connection, of our sharing our deepest feelings, thoughts and experiences and because we are in communion with each other that I'm not LONELY. Oh, I still miss her physical presence - her touch, her kiss, her words. I note with some surprise that being entwined with Pat in my dreams helps with this to a large degree.

Monday April 10, 2017 at 8 am:
Loves grows

Working on 'Quiet Love' I saw in Pat's diaries how over the years our love grew stronger and stronger and we two grew more alike. It helped that we started out very alike. She started out as a better person than I as well as a happier person. I think I grew both in caring and happiness. But Pat wasn't always pleased especially when she saw some of my mother creeping around in me. In middle age Pat seemed to pick up my melancholia and self doubt. I'm sorry I had that effect on the beautiful person she was. Now I feel she has peace even as she sometimes shows frustration with me. Pat, I love you forever!

Monday April 10, 2017 at 10 am
An observation

An observation: Though Pat is in heaven and outside time she is either not allowed to see the future inside time or not able to. It is no use us asking our loved ones about things in the future like when we will be joining them. The future remains not ours to see.

Monday April 10, 2017 at 8:30
Closure

Why would anyone seek closure? Why would anyone want to close the door on thoughts about a departed loved one? Grief will soften in the years after a loss, but the door to memories should always be open. Love is for all eternity and Love is stronger than Death. I hate people telling me to get over it. I don't want to get over it just to live with it. Pat, I love you forever. You are present in my heart and I shall eventually join you as one in Heaven.

Tuesday April 11, 2017 at 7:50
Reprogramming

All day today I've had this odd feeling. It is in my entire body - brain, head and chest. If I were a computer I'd say someone is reprogramming me updating all my software. Sure, hope it is either God or Patricia. It is draining me of all my energy and I don't want to do anything. My mind seems not to be able to get at my usual routines. All my hard disks are spinning. Feeling fearful, apprehensive, emotional and empty. Not depressed though. Interestingly I'm better able to visualize Pat's image in my minds eye - the graphics card seems to be working better. Now that is one improvement I approve of. God or Pat all this has to be for the good and for love. Wonder if I'm being born again. Definitely going to Mass tomorrow; maybe will get some answers during the meditation and prayers before communion.

Tuesday April 11, 2017 at 9:50
Incomplete

The loss of a spouse makes you feel entirely alone and
incomplete. The sense of feeling like you have lost an
essential part of yourself is both painful and
disconcerting. The world suddenly looks like a different
place, often odd and distanced. You are not sure how to
cope with life in general, and sometimes you may even
wonder if you even want to try. Reading over the
solemnisation of matrimony does provide closure if you
believe the meaning of this sacrament; God has joined
twain into one for all eternity. You really haven't lost your
spouse you have gained Christ. You are one with your
spouse in the arms of Christ in Heaven and she is still one
with you in your heart.

Wednesday April 11, 2017 at9:30am
It is different

I believe the death of a spouse is truly different from the
loss of any other family member. But I believe in the
sacrament of marriage where God joins two entities into
one and that although, death separates the physical
entities, the spiritual entity made by God remains united;
half in my heart the other half in heaven. I believe this
with all my being; I really haven't lost Patricia I have
gained Christ; I am one with her in the arms of Christ in

Heaven and she is still one with me in my heart. Now that should bring closure and great joy, right? So, why am I still grieving? I want her touch, kisses and words now more than ever. The tears are mostly for the loss of these. I rejoice in her PEACE and in the prospect of once again being fully one with her in Heaven

Thursday April 12, 2017 at 7 pm
Our Eternal Marriage

Patricia and I were two halves that together complete wholeness. Pat and I were the starting point in the sacrament of marriage where God joins two entities into one. When something is whole, it is unchanging and complete. So, when, death separates the physical entities into two halves - half in my heart, the other half in heaven, it upsets the equilibrium of wholeness and causes the pain of grief as both halves chase after each other as they seek a new balance with each other. We will not be fully whole again until we both are fully one in Heaven. In the meantime, I repeat, I really haven't lost Patricia I have gained Christ and am with Pat in the arms of Christ in Heaven and she is still one with me in my heart.
The Bible says "So God created man in His own image, in the image of God He created him; male and female He created them. (Genesis 1:27). It is not the physical body God "made" in His image but the soul and love. Men and women were created in the image of God the Father and

the Son by the Holy Ghost, a human body is not essential to image bearing. It is the identity we feel in our loved one's presence that is created in God's image. Marriage was also created in His Image. When we marry, we become a three in one united soul - Pat, I and our Love, three persons, the image of the divine Trinity. I rejoice in her PEACE and in the prospect of once again being fully one with her in Heaven.

When Pat was alive we worked for the good of each other. We never shut each other out. In Pat's words, we were "communicating bubbles". She thought our marriage type, two intersecting circles, was the best type of marriage. She wrote, "I think we have learned to be kind to each other. A little wary of each other's privacy, but still touching." Our quiet love was a communion, a sharing of the wonders of the three persons (Pat, I and Love). We were most usually together and always aware of each other. We held hands not only when she was 64 but right to the end. We rested with our heads on each other's shoulders. Our souls were united even then; yes, we had true love – it conformed to and revealed each other's soul. It flowed from our decision to become One, as per our marriage vows. Love was the very center of our personal lives.

This type of love extends beyond the grave especially as Christ defeated Death. Okay the one left behind is incomplete, hurting and no longer whole. But there is still communion. Communion flows from the loved one in

Heaven to the grieving one still in the physical world. It is the third entity, Love, continuing to love and to restore the balance between Pat and me. We are still growing in Love and becoming that eternal united One, a union that will endure beyond the grave. A union of intellect, identity, attention and souls – a union with God.

I believe when I join Pat in Heaven we will be born again as a united eternal soul (three persons in one), a new unit of wholeness but still a trinity – Pat I and Love. Already I feel Pat becoming stronger in me.

Good Friday 2017 at 2 pm
Praying for heaven

Why do people worry when you speak, fantasise, or write about wanting to die? Easter, of all times of the year, is a time surely when it is permissible to want to die. Christ's resurrection gave us all something to look forward to, our own resurrection. The very thought should make you "feel good" and may also give an "atmosphere of growth" to your life, a way out of grief, because the future seems bright. The ad for 'The Kennedys: After Camelot' (an American television drama) has Jackie asking a priest if it is wrong to pray for death. I would answer that no it isn't wrong; Simeon did it and even Christ asked for this cup to be taken from him. Speaking, fantasising or writing about wanting to die DOES NOT mean you are about to commit suicide. I have a 95-year-old friend who lost her special

love a few years ago, who wants to join him in heaven
and finds talking about this very comforting. I am sure she
will not commit suicide. She has medical problems and
has signed a 'No Heroic Measure' document but that is as
far as she will go. She is happy but, like me sometimes
melancholy. She has great grand children and would
never do anything to hurt them. I too would never do
anything to hurt my grandchildren. Pat would not allow
me to hurt them. Please let us have our dreams of reunion
with our loved ones; we need them to handle our grief.

Saturday April 15, 2017 at 10 pm
Sacrament of marriage

It seems I am not getting through to many what I mean
when I say I believe the death of a spouse is truly
different from the loss of any other family member. I
found that those who understood were either High
Anglicans or Catholics. So, I looked up what the Catholic
Church had to say about marriage.
In the Catechism of the Catholic Church it is explained
that "the intimate community of life and love which
constitutes the married state has been established by the
Creator and endowed by him with its own proper laws.
God himself is the author of marriage." The vocation to
marriage is written in the very nature of man and woman
as they came from the hand of the Creator. " By reason of
their state in life and of their order, Christian spouses have

their own special gifts in the People of God. "This grace proper to the sacrament of Matrimony is intended to perfect the couple's love and to strengthen their indissoluble unity. By this grace, they "help one another to attain holiness in their married life and in welcoming and educating their children." Christ is the source of this grace. "Just as of old God encountered his people with a covenant of love and fidelity, so our Savior, the spouse of the Church, now encounters Christian spouses through the sacrament of Matrimony. "Christ dwells with them, gives them the strength to take up their crosses and so follow him, to rise again after they have fallen, to forgive one another, to bear one another's burdens" "and to love one another with supernatural, tender, and fruitful love"

Wow that is right on. It is what I've been trying to say. In the sacrament of marriage God joins two entities into one. The term "one flesh" means that just as our bodies are one whole entity and cannot be divided into pieces and still be a whole, so God intended it to be with the marriage relationship. There are no longer two entities (Though there are still two persons), but now there is one entity (a married couple). There are a number of aspects to this union. First and foremost, our identity is bound with one another, the identity of each is united in the identity of the marriage. The death of a spouse is truly different from the loss of any other family member; the spiritual entity made by God remains united; half in my heart the other half in heaven. I believe this with all my being; I really haven't lost Patricia I have gained Christ; I am one with her in the arms of Christ in Heaven and she is still one with me in my heart.

God has a higher calling for the marriage. Even as we were serving Christ with our lives before marriage, in marriage we served Christ together as a unit. I was joyful when Pat was confirmed and able to take communion beside me. As a couple pursues serving Christ together, the joy which the Spirit gives filled our marriage. In the Garden of Eden, there were three persons present (Adam, Eve, and God), and there was joy. So, if God is central in a marriage today, there also will be joy. Without God, a true and full oneness is not possible. C. S. Lewis understood this when he wrote to Sheldon Vanauken that Sheldon should work toward the perfect marriage, "GOD and US". I add, marriage is an earthly trinity – Pat, I and the third person, our Love. God created marriage in the image of the Trinity.

True Love in marriage forces us with all our being, to acknowledge in each other that same absolute central significance which, because of the power of our egos, we are conscious of only in our own selves – our very egos unite! Our identity, the very center of our personal being shifts to our marriage, this leads to the indissoluble union of two lives into one: only of it does the Bible say: "They shall be one flesh". And after death of both shall become united in one real eternal being. I repeat what I've said before: when, death separates the physical entities into two halves - half in my heart, the other half in heaven, it upsets the equilibrium of wholeness and causes the pain of grief as both halves chase after each other as they seek a new balance with each other. We will not be fully whole again until we both are fully one in Heaven.

Monday April 17, 2017 Easter Monday
Easter thoughts

Everyone says that in the grief journey, holidays are the worst. Well I had a lovely Easter. Good Friday, James and I enjoyed Beethoven's Missa Solemnis performed magnificently by the Grand Philharmonic Choir. Saturday was a good day too – breakfast with James and Nora, then over to their house to join Erin and Vivi and watch the granddaughter open Pat's and my Easter presents and eat lots of chocolate. In the afternoon, I walked one of Pat's favourite walks through the neighbourhood seeing lots of flowers in bloom. Quiet evening watching TV and reading. Sunday the big day - Acts 2:32 This Jesus God raised up, and of that all of us are witnesses - started by James and I attending the 11 am service at Holy Saviour. Fr. Carver's sermon was very moving; all about how Love is stronger than Death a topic you all know I've been thinking about a lot. The Communion was also very movingly done by The Venerable Cy Ladds who was obviously moved by it too. After Mass, I drove out to visit Pat and put flowers on Pat's grave for Easter. Prayed: May

Patricia evermore dwell in me and I in her through Jesus
Christ. Amen. On way back home had coffee and a lovely
chat with the owner of Angie's Waterloo about Pat and
picked up a fresh loaf of bread for Easter Dinner. Brought
over to James and Erin's my contributions to our Easter
Dinner - sirloin tip pot roast, the bread, French rhubarb
custard pie and a bottle of wine. Rosemarie and Michael
contributed very good mashed potatoes and lots of
candies and presents for the girls. We didn't talk about Pat
so as not to disturb the granddaughters. It was a very
pleasant weekend all in all and not at all hard for me.
It is only when you have great expectations that it gets
hard. Well I did have great expectations. Easter is about
Love conquering Death and about the Resurrection. I was
expecting a break-through in my communications with
Pat and a strengthening of our communion with each
other. That was my deepest silent prayer. By bed time
nothing had happened but I still had hopes. Even went to
bed early in hopes of a dream revelation.
Did I ever have a bad night! Those were not dreams or
revelations I had. My night was filled with nightmares
and not a bit of the Love I was expecting. The nightmares
brought back everything I felt during the first few days
after she died; grief had come full circle. There was the
fear but, this time I was truly afraid. I thought Pat's Real
Presence was leaving me. A couple of the bad dreams
were about Pat breaking up with me, abandoning me,
changing her phone number so I couldn't find her.

Changing her appearance so I wouldn't recognize her. (She had painted a third eye in the middle of her forehead in one dream; just like you sometimes see in fortune teller posters.) Yes, I felt great anger at this abandonment. And I felt the great loss again. I was very much alone in my dreams. I felt abandoned by everybody and everything – where was that great comforter whose resurrection we had celebrated Easter Day. Here I was for most of the night in HELL. Was Christ showing me what He experienced when He descended into hell?

All this because I got greedy in my wants and expectations. I don't want the sense of Pat's presence to disappear in a second death; I want it to last forever. I just wanted it to be stronger. I wanted to hear her words again and feel her kisses. My love for her has not died, it shall continue forever. I must learn patience; the real presence and our love is growing and I just have to wait. Time has no relevance to her (or God) in eternity. She is still in my heart and her presence IS still getting stronger. O Lord, I most humbly beseech thee of thy great goodness to comfort and succour me in this transitory life and give me the grace to rejoice in Pat's fellowship in Heaven and in my heart. Amen.

Monday April 17, 2017
How do I love thee?

Just when I'm feeling really low something comes up to remind me of how much she loves me. The sound of her voice calling "Eric" to wake me after a noon nap. And now I find a note on a 3 x 5 scrap of paper which she must have written in early December pinned on my bulletin board just behind my monitor. She wrote "Eric, I love you forever." Tears of happiness. Pat, I love you forever too! Can there be any doubt that we will unite into one soul in Heaven when my time comes? Lord let me evermore dwell in Pat and her in me in the grace of Christ. Amen.

Tuesday April 18, 2017 at 7:20 am
Life after death

I started reading Tom Harper's 'There is life after death' his revision and expansion of 'Life after death' I had read years ago. Interesting that so often spouses that have an after-death experience and/or feel the presence of their departed, begin their account with the statement that they were "always very happy together." They do not mention their love though you can see it in the way the experience is described. I believe great love is required to have such an experience. The other thing many of them have in common is they are usually awakened from a sound sleep. Such was the case with my first experience of Pat's presence. I had stretched out on the living room couch planning to nap until the news came on. I fell into a sound sleep but soon felt someone standing bent over me and kissing me on the lips; it caused me to wake up and I clearly saw Pat. I tried to touch her and kiss back but the image started to fade and she was gone. I felt good about the experience and knew it was really her comforting me. I think she was forgiving me for being in another room not holding her hand when she departed. It was NOT a dream but a very real experience of life after death. I also think I can be sure that when I die she will be there holding my hand to help me across. Pat, I love you for ever! Thank you.

Wednesday April 18, 2017 at 1 pm
Entwined together

Why do I feel so lonely? I desperately yearn for Pat's physical company. Oh, I feel her Real presence and I am in communion with her; the result of me dwelling in her and she dwelling in me. There are pictures of her in every room and I walk around talking to her. Why isn't this enough?
We are born into a physical world and are dependant on our senses to relate to that world. We are bombarded by sight, hearing, touching, smelling and tasting. We can't cope without at least some of these stimulations from the physical world. They drown out the spiritual; that is why we have so much trouble meditating and communing with God. I am physically alone (except for the friendly new tabby replacing Pooka) but still hear the traffic which

draws me out of my meditations. What I miss is the physical her – the her I became dependant on in 48 years of marriage. I am sure Pat understood this when she wished to live the life of a hermit with me beside her. I'm scared to admit it but, she probably would be happier in my present situation than I am: it is very much like the hermit life with the silent, physically unseen and unheard presence of my spouse within me.

Loneliness is being alone when you desire otherwise. I desperately want Patricia - her words, her touch, her kisses, her physical being - back. So, I am lonely. That is the very definition of being lonely. It is a desolate feeling of being left behind, and being all alone forever. There is a Pat sized hole in my heart, which I cannot live with or without. It is all my memories of Patricia which I never want to lose. Those memories are happy memories though I cry.

In our marriage, there was a deep inner sense of a quiet deep love at its centre. It continues as the uninterrupted center of both of us. Our love continues to grow stronger. To the doubter, NO I don't need to get over my grief and pass on: Pat and I love each other forever, ours is an eternal marriage. Love is stronger than death. Not everything ends in death. Our marriage is Pat and I and us. Marriage is created in the image of God. In heaven, Pat and I will be truly like the triune God – a trinity. Christ's resurrection did not end his love for the Father, it strengthens the Holy Ghost or so I believe.

Pat's 12th Anniversary Poem says it all:
I know the scent and shape of you:
I know you all, yet not at all.
I linger with a connoisseur's delight
over a contour of bone, a texture of skin,
gloating over treasures of silk and ivory
that are mine alone,
and yet no-one's but yours.

For you and I are so entwined
that we can read each other's mind
at times, a simple exercize.
Then comes the stumble of surprise
when, reaching out in haste, I find
the stranger self behind your eyes.

Far apart upon the lawn,
two tall trees confront each other
never to touch, ever alone:
yet beneath the grass and stone
intertwined their roots have grown,
so intimately webbed together,
neither one can tell his own.

So with us: which flatly proves
futility of arguments
On which is which, and whose is whose.

We are the one eternal united entity we vowed to become in our marriage vows. Pat and I love each other forever. No, I won't be lonely forever. That will disappear when we are united in Heaven.

Thursday April 20 at 4:09pm
Papacy on united resurrection entity·

According to the Pontifical Household preacher, Capuchin Father Raniero Cantalamessa, marriage does not come to a complete end at death but is transfigured, spiritualized, freed from the limits that mark life on earth, as also the ties between parents and children or between friends will not be forgotten. In a preface for the dead the liturgy proclaims: "Life is transformed, not taken away." Even marriage, which is part of life, will be transfigured, not nullified. I take great comfort in this.

Friday April 21, 2017 at 9:30
Meditations

Woke up just before 5 am for the usual reason. Got back in bed and couldn't get back to sleep. So, I lay on my back and found a comfortable position with no stress or tension in my body. Emptied my mind so my mind's eye was seeing only black darkness. Breathed in and out just feeling the movement of my in and out breaths. And repeated in my mind "May Pat every more dwell in me and I in her." The house was quiet except for the clock ticking and chiming the half hours and hours. A great calm came over me. Then the blackness changed to a light sky-blue colour with powder white stylized birds - just like Pat's favourite jersey. It pulsed in time to my breathing. Shortened the manta to just her name, Pat. A new pulsating colour appeared – a light yellow green moving through the powdery blue like the oil in those old Lava lights pulsed through the water. Blue and yellow forever individual but occupying the same space. I began to think I felt Pat's presence – that the light blue was her and the light oily yellow-green was me. I was at peace and felt rested. When I heard, the paper being put in my mail box I decided to get up. It was after 7 am. Okay this proves nothing except that I can meditate. However, I believe it was Pat and I; we were doing a marriage dance: you know that feeling, you are dancing inside and have an eternal connection to your loved one and all we have to do is think of them, pray with them to Christ, love them, meditate, live, breathe them in, and they are there again. Love is stronger than Death and Pat and I love each other forever!

Sunday April 23, 2017 at 4 pm.
Why?

Why? This is a question without an answer. Things don't happen because it is God's Will. We have free will and live in a world that obeys the laws of science - okay that could be God's Will. It is still a violent world and we still have free will. There is nobody to blame. Life is life. God so loved the world, that he gave his only begotten Son, to the end that all that believe him should not perish, but have eternal life. That is our comfort. The END is not the END but a new beginning.

Monday April 24. 2007 at noon
Sweet spot

Partners in healthy, happy relationships find a balance between wanting to be with their partner and needing to be with them. Pat and I found that sweet spot, that balance. It is what quiet love is all about- Pat's touching circles. Pat and I didn't have to worry about losing each other because we love each other forever. Our marriage united us into one entity forever. Mind you the grief still came and still hurt. Pray for those that have lost their faith as well as a loved one - belief that Love is stronger than Death and that God is LOVE are a necessity for comfort.

Tuesday April 25, 2017 at 8 pm
Snuggling with Pat

Feeling a bit down this morning because of rain and missing Pat. Felt Pat's presence and she suggested a cuddle in my mind. Well, I was a bit doubtful but I snuggled up to her pillow (it still has her lavender sachet inside the case) and suddenly it was like she was there as she was so many nights in our 48 years. I fit perfectly against her and I had a very comforting and refreshing nap. Felt a whole lot better when I awoke. Guess I'll include this in my REAL presence experiences of her.

Friday April 28, 2017 at 5 pm
Real presence

"Please God let me see her real resurrection body and not the ashes." My prayer was answered. Today's nap brought Pat's presence. At first, she gave me a slide show of recent images of herself based on my favourite pictures of her ending with the one of her knitting in the hospital. Then I was looking at her as she is now. She is far more beautiful than any of these images. She is perfect. Age, sickness and Death have not touched her; She is healthy and though an adult she looks young, vibrant and beautiful. She still has the perfect complexion the PSWs and nurses all commented on. There was also a radiance to her like polished gold. She communicated " You have eyes to see; so, see me now as I am awaiting thee." The image grew life sized and I knew it was her REAL presence. God does answer our prayers and LOVE is stronger than Death. Pat, I love you forever.

Saturday April 29, 2017
My Grief Journey.

In writing Quiet Love, writing for my blog, and posting
on Facebook, I have been working out my beliefs on life
after death and on love and marriage. I have been reading
Sheldon Vanauken, C. S. Lewis, Cynthia Bourgeault,
Tom Harper, various essays on the topics found by
Google and reading quite a few poets and of course
reading Pat's poems and 48 years of her diaries. In the
four months after Pat's death I have healed somewhat
because of this research and my writing about my feelings
and developing beliefs and with the help of family and
friends. What surprises me most is that Pat came to these
same conclusions in her journals long before I ever
thought of them. They were in her diaries and poems for
me to find. Her REAL Presence was also guiding me to
what she had found. Her Christianity was much further
along than mine. At times, I felt her annoyance at my not
"getting it" and she would snap an "of course I love you"
at me or an "of course I'm here in your heart" at me.
Pat often went for walks where she wanted and needed to
be alone. I just discovered from her 2016 diary that she
usually prayed at the Canadiana Garden Park at Shephard
School or the Women's War Memorial garden in front of
the armory. She always took a break there to think about
herself and to pray for forgiveness for her sins and relief
from her faults. Also from the 2016 diary, she was often

up between 4 am and 5 am depressed at what she thought of as her short comings and sins and thinking and praying for forgiveness and solutions. Seems she was on an inner journey much like I have been since her death. There are, between 2007 and 2012, even passages in her diaries where she describes exactly the great grief I went though - am still at times experiencing. I believe it was these times of deep thought and prayer that she came to the conclusions I have been coming to about love, marriage, God and death. In diary entries after writing about her depression she often wrote about her insights. She also occasionally nuzzled me awake to talk about them.

So, what have Pat and I learnt in all this thought, prayer, reading and research? Pat and I believe Christ's promise that there is a place in Heaven for each of us believers prepared by Christ himself. We also believe the New Testament passages promising we will recognize our loved ones even in their new eternal Christ-like body and that our loved ones will be waiting for us when we get to heaven to help our rebirth into the eternal resurrection body. I believe I saw the resurrected Pat after noon on Friday April 28, 2017 – she was beautiful and radiant. Pat and I also believed very strongly in the sacrament of marriage. Our marriage in St. Stephen's in the Fields Anglican Toronto lead into a full Mass. We believe that in marriage two entities are made one by God never to be separated even by death itself. Pat and I are still united - Pat dwelling in my heart and I dwelling in her in Heaven through Christ. In fact, we are made whole again by death. We also both believe that love continues after death and continues to grow every stronger. As described by Pat, though we are two individuals we are still united as we were on earth. We are a trinity – Pat, I and the person that our love is. The third person, Love, is the binding force just like the Holy Ghost in the divine Trinity. Christians have always believed that God is Love and that LOVE is what unites us all in the communion of Saints. "For you must realize," says Jacob Boehme, (Confessions) "that earth unfolds its properties and powers in union with Heaven aloft above us, and there is one Heart, one Being, one Will, one God, all in all." On the Grief Journey, you eventually stop running and simply look in your own heart and are swallowed by the embrace of your loved one in her eternal resurrection body – you are united again in the love of Christ. You realize nothing has changed, you are whole again and nothing, no part of your love is taken away. You continue to grow in love forever. Enduring is part of Christian love, the love which brought Pat and I together in marriage. The end of the great journey is when you discover God has been calling you to become true man and wife united in one eternal resurrection body in Heaven. All you need is true love. I believe in our 48 years together we both dissolved and were born again in our marriage. We remained individuals – Pat's two touching circles - but our marriage was the wholeness of the us, True Love.

According to the Pontifical Household preacher, Capuchin Father Raniero Cantalamessa, marriage does not come to a complete end at death but is transfigured, spiritualized, freed from the limits that mark life on earth, as also the ties between parents and children or between friends will not be forgotten. In a preface for the dead the liturgy proclaims: "Life is transformed, not taken away." Even marriage, which is part of life, will be transfigured, not nullified. I take great comfort in this. Pat proved and I believe that LOVE is stronger than DEATH. Christ thoroughly defeated Death.

Sunday April 30, 2017 at 1:10 pm
Beliefs

I BELIEVE that neither death, nor life, nor angels, nor principalities, nor powers, nor things present, nor things to come, nor height, nor depth, nor any other thing, shall be able to separate us (that is Pat and I) from the love of God and from each other united in HOLY Matrimony. And I BELIEVE in the resurrection of the body, and the life of the world to come, through our Lord Jesus Christ; who shall change our mortal bodies into a resurrection body, that be like unto His glorious body. May Pat dwell in me and I in her though Christ forever. Amen

May

DEXTER'S MAZE
November 1993.
For 'The Spiral Maze'.

Ye who walk these branching ways,
warily and softly wend.
Time and chance make such a maze,
peril waits at ev'ry bend.

Here, no hope nor fear is vain.
Here, all dreams may yet come true.
Shades may live, and substance gain;
all things lost be found anew.

Yet wisely tread, or learn the cost:
that finder be forever lost.

Monday May 1, 2017 at 2:15
Grief strengthens faith

In Quiet Love, I wrote the following: "I have lost the
ability to enjoy all the things we enjoyed together; the
ability to enjoy every day's most common loves by sun or
candle light. Now I listen to a piece of music we once
enjoyed together and it sounds hollow. I look at a painting
we loved together and it just doesn't move me in the same
way it once did. A bright sunny day is not appreciated the
same. The atmosphere and food in one of our favourite
restaurants just is not as good anymore. A TV show we
both looked forward to now brings tears to my eyes. The
pleasure of cooking a great meal for supper is gone; it is
just food now. I feel like I have lost half of myself...."
In the four months since Pat's death, I still feel much the
same but maybe a bit less intensely. I am melancholy and
don't feel any purpose to doing any of the needed daily
chores. Oh, I do them because Pat would have wanted me
to but there is no urgency in me. However, there have
been gains – discovering how intensely and deeply we
love each other, and that Love continues to grow and
deepen after death. The biggest surprise was discovering
how deeply religious she was and is – she wanted to be
alone on her walks to meditate and pray. This has
strengthened my own faith as has finding her homemade
prayer/promise bracelet next to her laptop. I now wear it

daily. Daily prayer: "Lord let Pat forever more dwell in me and I in her through Christ our Lord. Amen." The Eternal promise: Pat, I love you forever! I am surer than ever that there is life after death and that our marriage is about our becoming a renewed united entity united by LOVE in the arms of Christ.

I still really want to join Pat in Heaven and still occasionally pray, "Oh God let my release be soon! Amen." But I realize that it is not going to be soon. Pat predicted in 2010 that neither of us would make it to 2020. Well she was right about herself, just hope she was right about me also. Like Pat I've had serious health problems in the last decade – seven ulcers two bleeding ones that put me in the hospital, high blood pressure for decades but under control, and a heart attack in 2015 that resulted in quintuple bypass open heart surgery. That is why I thought I would be first to die. Pat died just after her 70th birthday – the Biblical 3 score and 10. I wonder if my surviving these serious health problems means I am strong and will make it to the Biblical 4 score – I much prefer Pat's prediction obviously. The time of my death is not my choice but Gods. Wish I was a poet like Pat; melancholy and love result in great poems.

Monday May 1, 2017 at 8 pm
First time alone

It is very late to come to this conclusion, I am lonely
because this is the first time in 74 years that I have been
absolutely physically alone for such a time. The first 26
years of my life I lived with my parents; the next 48 years
I lived with Pat. Now though I feel Pat's spiritual presence
I am absolutely physically alone. It does not feel nice; I
need actual physical touching and communication. The
cat doesn't help much. Without Pat's physical presence I'm
even lonely in a crowded room. Loneliness hurts.

Monday May 1, 2017 at 8:30 pm
Touching

Couples who are very much in love frequently touch. If
you watch closely there is the small glancing brush of
flesh against flesh. hair brushing a cheek, head briefly
leaning on the others shoulder, the stolen kiss, etc.
Couples truly in love find innumerable ways to touch in
ways they think nobody will notice. It happens so often it
become a habit. Then there is the full-blown holding of
hands - yes, I was still holding Pat's hand at 74. This is
why I miss her so.

Tuesday May 2, 2017 at 2:30 pm
Want her presence

There are still people who tell me to "get over it", "keep busy so she's not always on my mind", "make new friends", etc. They don't seem to realize that I don't want to fill that deep, Pat sized hole; that is where she dwells in me. I don't ever want to forget her and I don't want the memories to fade. Just the opposite - I want her presence in me to grow ever stronger. I love Pat and I love feeling her in me. Even if it sometimes hurts and sometimes I cry and am always lonely. I repeat, I love Pat forever. Hey, there is NO time table for grief - everyone grieves in their own way and to their own time table. Everyone also grieves differently. Please remember I am surer than ever that there is life after death and that our marriage is about our becoming a renewed united entity united by LOVE in the arms of Christ. "Death is not extinguishing the light; it is only putting out the lamp because the dawn has come." - Rabindranath Tagore. Death is the beginning of a new day!

Wednesday May 3, 2017 at 7 am
Dream and waiting

Odd dream last night around 4 am. Pat and I had been working on something down the basement and there was sawdust all over. Well I swept up and when finished I went to go up the stairs and found Pat had painted the stairs and the paint was still wet. I yelled up to her; she replied, "You will just have to wait." Woke up and went to WC. Back to sleep until regular get up time. In the haze between sleep and awake I saw Pat's computer screen as I often do. There was a message on it. Something about her getting my message about the new school arrangements, a http address which I don't remember and some more stuff about preparing a place. It ended with the symbol for a prescription (R with a slash through the front leg) followed by "Accept" another http address I don't remember and "You'll just have to wait." She is really emphasizing my waiting. Pat, I get the message – I am waiting even if it is impatiently.

Wednesday May 3, 2017 at 8:45 am
Meeting me half way

I do not have to come all the way to Pat in Heaven, because she is also coming to me. I already have that empty hole in me to let her in. We are still two individuals united into one trinity by marriage and love. My dream and message last night shows that nothing has changed. She still gets annoyed with me, still loves me and still nags me. Our love is still growing stronger as is her presence in me. Pat is not here physically and that does make me feel lonely but, our most precious memories are

149

still within me and it is easier now to call them up at well. Pat, I love you forever.

Thursday May 4, 2017 at 9 am
One in Marriage for all eternity

In thinking back to how Pat and I spent our life together, I realized just how little we talked. Talk was mostly about day to day things like: what do you want for breakfast; what did you and James talk about at lunch, is this a laundry day, what do we need in groceries, where do you want to celebrate this anniversary, etc. There was a lot of touching, working side by side on our computers, (Pat wrote that she felt closest to me when we were both working on our computers side by side; I think that is why she now often communicates with me in the haze of waking from sleep on a big white computer screen.) reading side by side, side by side at Tai Chi, and watching TV. But very little talking about the deep issues of life. At Church, we enjoyed the service together often touching hands and meditated together during communion. Yes, we communicated but it was somehow beyond words. Pat said it best: "For you and I are so entwined / that we can read each other's mind / at times, a simple exercize. / Then comes the stumble of surprise / when, reaching out in haste, I find / the stranger self behind your eyes." Our love grew ever stronger as did our faith even without the constant chatter some couples constantly insist on. We

were happy in our quiet love and in just having each other
near. We were most together in our thoughts and minds.
Pat wrote a lot of her deepest thoughts down in her dairies
and journals. That is how I discovered in researching for
"Quiet Love" that she was further along than I in
understanding our love, marriage and faith. Also, being a
poet and novelist, she was more open to both nature and
God. I must think deeply about things, brood over them,
meditate on them and wait for my subconscious to come
up with the things Pat just seemed to know. Our union
into one entity in marriage caused both of us to grow in
love and faith. We are still growing. As friends and family
saw we were a very together couple. We were in marriage
already one entity or at least there was a third entity
always present in us together – the one created by the
sacrament of marriage. It was and is as if our minds were
working out the answers together. Thoughts like these are
much more than words, they are feelings, our very soul
and LOVE. As a friend recently commented "Love for
one's spouse is the same as love for God." We absorbed
each others' truths directly, we had in Pat's words, "eyes
to see and words to tell the truths that are most true." To
friends, family, and others, we were probably "cute" (look
at those old folks holding hands) and boring. What we
have is Quiet Love that is eternal. Again, from that friend,
we "live with the memories and the hopes and dreams we
create together and hope to share in our eternal life in
Christ." I shall love Pat forever.

Friday May 5, 2017 at 10:45 am
Greatest Fear

Two years after his wife's death, Vanauken wrote: "…I found that my tears were dried. The grief had passed…. There was no sense of Davy's being there with me, nor any sense that she was in the wind…. There were no more dreams…. This – the disappearance of the sense of the beloved's presence and, therefore, the end of tears – this is the Second Death." This "Second Death" is the point of the title of his book, "A Severe Mercy; a story of faith, tragedy, and triumph."

I fear this severe mercy above all else. C. S. Lewis, after his experience of Joy's presence, wrote in "A Grief observed", "It was quite incredibly unemotional. Just the impression of her mind momentarily facing my own…. Yet, there was an extreme and cheerful intimacy. An intimacy that had not passed though the senses or emotions at all…. The intimacy was complete – sharply bracing and restorative too – without it." His wife, Joy, died less than a year before he wrote this and he had bone cancer himself. He asked his wife on her death bed "If you can - if it is allowed - come to me when I too am on my death bed." She had promised and I believe the presence he felt was the beginning of her keeping her promise. I think Lewis also did not want "severe mercy." Unlike Vanauken he needed Joy's presence and the promise that she would be there holding his hand at the end. He continues "There is also, whatever it means, the resurrection of the body. We cannot understand. The best is perhaps what we understand least." I probably have longer than Lewis had when he accepted Joy's presence but not the nearly 40 years from Vanauken's time of his severe mercy, the second death, to his death. Never-the-less, please God no "Severe Mercy" for me. I need and want Pat's presence dwelling in me forever as well as the promise of her being with me holding my hand when my time comes.

As I wrote in *Quiet Love …. Eyes to see and words to tell the truths that are most true*, "Patricia and I were lucky enough to discover that quiet, intense love that is basic to life itself; it is seldom found in real life. We had the eyes to see and the words to tell the truths that are most real to each other." It is the kind of love Cynthia Bourgeault, in her *Love is stronger than Death; the mystical union of two souls*, was describing when she wrote: "In certain, perhaps rare, love relationships, instead of the normal imperative for letting go and getting on with life, there are subtle but clear signs that the journey with one's beloved continues beyond the grave. Rather than ending, the walk together is only just getting under way….it also happens to real people. I know this because I am one of them." Well I think Pat and I are also one of them. Right from the beginning we found God in our lives – He answered a prayer of mine when Pat became the first girl to come to Church with me. We made our marriage vows to God and to each other. We vowed to forgive one another, to bear one another's burdens, to be subject to one another out of reverence for Christ, and to love one another with supernatural, tender, and fruitful love.

In the first few weeks after Pat's death I stumbled about in the numbness of grief. I felt empty. As Pat wrote in her dairy, "There was a kind of confusion about death itself - it's impossible to understand of course. Like a rabbit in a magicians' trick. Where did it go? The body remains, but the real woman has vanished!... I don't believe that the live soul simply stops existing. It did exist; therefore, it still exists. Where? I suppose one must think in terms of heaven since one must visualize something…. Perhaps it is enough simply to believe the spirit does not die." We both had read Tom Harpur's *There is Life after Death* and we are also sure that there is life after death. Harpur wrote "…But I assure you that I am convinced of this as I am of anything in this world: a day is coming when all separations will be over. We will one day be reunited (in the words of the old hymn) with "whom we have loved long since and lost a while." We will return to the source of our being, not as rivers return to the ocean and are swallowed by it, but as recognizable individuals."

I am also convinced of the truth of Bourgeault's experiences described in her book and think Pat and I are on a similar journey to our reunion in the arms of Christ. Bourgeault wrote: "I see the body of hope as a living, palpable, and conscious energy that holds the visible and invisible worlds together. It is the sap, metaphorically speaking, through which flows the higher communion – the sharing of personal love and the building up and unfolding of the wonders between two people. It is what makes possible the communion of substances between two beloveds and the continuing growth of their one abler soul even when separated by death. It is the "holy element," as Boehme would call it, that straddles heaven and earth and makes possible the most intimate connection between these two planes."

I believe that my three experiences of communicating with Pat in the week after she died were the beginning of an experience similar to Bourgeault's. It is not something that will end like Vanauken's experiences. The fact that I have had other such experiences of Pat's presence, communications, dreams, is evidence that our love is growing and we will reunite in one soul in Heaven. No Severe Mercy is needed or wanted, thank you very much.

Saturday May 6, 2017 at 2 pm
Separation trauma

On Saturday, December 3, 1988 Pat wrote after a three day stay in Toronto General for an operation and on learning of my two sleepless nights: "I think we've reached the point in our marriage when separation is a trauma." Well she was right, the "trauma" occurred every time to the one left at home during the other's stays in the

155

hospital. And it wasn't just for operations – I got it when she went to Montreal to visit her dying mother. During my heart attack in 2015 Pat didn't get much sleep during all the time I was in St. Mary's. It explains the great loneliness the one in hospital feels at night for her loved one; Pat used to wait for me by the elevator in the mornings before breakfast arrived. I had separation trauma after her death; it is a big part of the Grief Journey. I believe at some point in the 19th year of our marriage we truly became one entity. Our souls became so intertwined, so intimately webbed together that neither of us could tell which was which, and whose was whose. Yes, we suffered trauma on separation and death is a separation. At least until I found her dwelling in me and I dwelling in her. Maybe the grief therapists should consider treating Grief as PSTD.

Monday May 8, 2017
My companion and best friend

While most of the grief is for Pat as my wife and other half; my grief also includes the loss of Pat as my best friend and companion. I miss most going to a BCP coral mass with her. Also miss being her caregiver when she was sick; it was hard work but there is something special about being able to help your loved one and to fulfill her wishes. Missing the companionship is what makes me most lonely and sad - Pat and I were very close and no one can replace her in this role. Pat, I love you forever.

Tuesday May 9, 2017
Home

Her first December (1991) in Kitchener, Pat, wrote after a RWA lunch in Toronto: " I felt no connection to the place at all. I haven't missed Toronto since we left it (I know Eric has) and I'm not sure it's because I feel more at home here or because I'm not at home anywhere." (After the 2003 vacation in Nova Scotia she felt herself a Maritimer and dreamt of returning there.) For me, home is where the heart is and that is where Pat is. She is in her true home now and I hope happy and comfortable there in the arms of Christ. May Pat ever dwell in me and I in her and may I return home to her soon through Christ. Amen.

May 11, 2017
Not suicidal

Why do people, even doctors, think praying for death is a mental illness? Heaven and joining your loved one there is a beautiful thought; as well as being very comforting. Simeon and Christ where not mentally ill. Nor are the theologians who write about life after death. Okay being suicidal is an illness. But there is a big difference between thinking about the joy and love in Christ's arms and being suicidal. We Christians say we "look for the Resurrection of the dead" in the creed we say in Church. Don't councillors and mental health specialists believe in Christ's victory over death? From personal experience, I know how very comforting it is if your doctor is a Christian and welling to talk to you about your and his belief in Christ and life after death.

I had a check-up yesterday and I'm fine thank you. I also had such a chat with my Doctor, a Christian and received great comfort from it.

Sunday May 14, 2017
In His image:

JOHN 14:2 KJV: In my Father's house are many mansions: if [it was] not [so], I would have told you. I go to prepare a place for you.

Learned in Church today that this is, word for word, what the Hebrew bridegroom of Biblical times said in his betrothal covenant. It ended with them sealing their vow by sharing a glass of wine. The groom then went off to actually build a room onto his parent's home. When finished, he came back to get his bride. Can there be any doubt that God created man AND women in his own image (So God created mankind in his own image, in the image of God he created them; male and female he created them.) and thus it is the single married entity that was created in God's image - not the individual man and

158

woman... And with these words and the last supper's
bread and wine, Christ was making a covenant with Man"

Monday ay 15, 2017 at 8:45 am
Pat communes with me

Okay I give up; can't find the answer to my question so,
I'm going with Psychology Today's: "So, from the
viewpoint of the mourner experiencing an EE, the
question "Is it real, or is it hallucination?" is not the issue.
Just like with the wine glass in the Memorex ad, it makes
no difference - it's the same result! Assuming the mourner
is not severely agitated or suffering from deep emotional
trauma at the time of the event, the real issue is what
impact EEs have. For nearly all mourners, they are
comforting, authentic, and life enriching."
It helps me to believe that Pat is communicating with me
and for me her presence feels as real as the presence of
Christ at Holy Communication. I believe Pat dwells in me
and I dwell in her and her presence in me is getting
stronger as is my love for her. C.S. Lewis, Sheldon
Vanauken, Cynthia Bourgeault, Tom Harper and of
course both Saints Peter and Paul believed in the Real
Presence and so do I.

Tuesday May 16, 2017
Untitled poem by Eric Bow (1969)

Come walk with me;
talk with me
of loneliness,
of dying,
the need for crying.

Believe
not to argue
or explain.

Can you relate,
communicate,
bring two brings into one?

I talk of things I shall never see,
kings unborn and the false me,
I open a door here and there,
Is it me that you see;
The me crying out my need?
I am lonely, I am sad.
The music that I play,
is it me;
can I be?
Am I ...
a collage of false images and other people's dreams?

I do not know what I want,
what I will be,
the Mongol khan,
the conqueror,
the meek,
the peacemaker.
Just me alone,
unable to communicate
relate
belong.
The empty void within,
crying to the empty void without.

Wednesday May 17, 2017
Another poem of mine from 1968 Pat kept.

God – the way, impalpable, invisible

He sees me, has seen me and ever shall see me;
His eyes penetrate the very essence of my being
Before the wondrous process of my creation began.
Where can I escape his watchful eye:
Where do I travel to escape my destiny?
I hide in darkness, yet the dark does not hide me,
He is there, he is there to comfort me, to guide my
footsteps.

I demand the impossible, I demand divine favour;
"Show me that I'm important," I cry,

"Respond thou faceless, cold, indifferent master."
He responds, not for me, for my soul.
He has searched me, known me, known my inner most
thoughts.
He leads me out of the valley of death: I drink the honey
of truth.

I cry, "Vanity of vanities, all is vanity: a world of
depression, a world of joys,
What profit either? One to the other returns; there is no
permanence."
He answers, "Serve me, love me, accept me and my
plans."
Where can I go to escape him; how can I not obey?
He is everywhere, he is everywhere.

I descend into hell and he is there;
I ascend into heaven and he is there.
Hell, heaven, they are the lot of man;
They praise the glory of God's name.
How can I not obey him? He is within me;
I hear his voice in my pleasure at a deed,
I hear his voice in my discomfort at evil.

How precious are thy thoughts to me, O God!
How great is the sum of them?
Thy Word is my way, the lamp of my feet;
Thy world magnifies thy name!

May 20, 2017
Grief has taught me

Between Patricia's death January 7, 2017 and Mothers'
Day, 2017 the most important thing I have learned is God
helps those who are seeking him. Grief is God shouting
at us. "God whispers in our pleasures, speaks in our
consciences, but shouts in our pains. It is his megaphone
to rouse a deaf world." – C. S. Lewis. Pat and I had been
seeking him for the 48 years of our marriage, we found
Him. Pat is in the arms of Christ preparing that place for
us that Christ promised. She was accepted into His arms
when her soul left her body. Resurrection and final
judgment take place immediately after death. As St. Paul
says, "To be absent from the body, is to be present with
the Lord." II Corinthians 5.
Pat is in Christ's arms as am I. Yes, I believe this: Pat
and I are not even separated by the death, since the spirit
of Pat continues to live in me. And this shall continue
until my death, when we meet again and reunite ourselves
and love each other more tenderly than before because we
are in the Great Now. I also believe our love is
continuing to grow ever stronger. The Torah says, "Male
and female He created them" (Genesis 1:27). ... Marriage
is the unification of two halves into one complete entity,
described as "one flesh." Christianity adds, that the
purpose of a marriage of one male and one female is to
unite them into one entity – it is in marriage that two are

163

joined as one in the image of the triune God. By marriage, the husband and wife are one person thus with marriage are a trinity.

On April 28 at 5:01pm I wrote on Facebook: "Please God let me see her real resurrection body and not the ashes." My prayer was answered. Today's nap brought Pat's presence. At first, she gave me a slide show of recent images of herself based on my favourite pictures of her ending with the one of her knitting in the hospital. Then I was looking at her as she is now. She is far more beautiful than any of these images. She is perfect. Age, sickness and Death have not touched her; She is healthy and though an adult she looks young, vibrant and beautiful. She still has the perfect complexion the PSWs and nurses all commented on. There was also a radiance to her like polished gold. She communicated " You have eyes to see so see me now as I am awaiting thee." The image grew life sized and I knew it was her REAL presence. God does answer our prayers and LOVE is stronger than Death. Pat, I love you forever.

Interestingly there was no awareness of time or physical space. Her glowing body was like a hologram as if made of light made solid in a Star Trek Holodeck. She was recognizable just as Christ was to his disciples but it was not a recreation of her old body. It was a spiritual body and perfect for her. I believe there is no time in Heaven. 2 Peter 3:8 King James Version 8. "But, beloved, be not ignorant of this one thing, that one day is with the Lord as a thousand years, and a thousand years as one day." For Pat, it will not be long before I join her. As Albert Einstein said, "the distinction between past, present and future is only an illusion." Pat is in the Great Now. "God is Light. Well over two thousand years ago, the prophet wrote: "Arise, shine: for thy light is come... The sun shall be no more thy light by day; neither for brightness shall the moon give light unto thee: but the Lord shall be unto thee an everlasting light and thy God thy glory. -- Tom Harpur. "Death is not extinguishing the light; it is only putting out the lamp because the dawn has come." — Rabindranath Tagore. These past 4.5 months, while at times very painful have taught me a lot about God, love and my wife Pat. I see clearly the eternal elements of our marriage and quiet love. I believe Cynthia Bourgeault when she tells of her continuing love beyond the grave and her 'Mystical Union of Two Souls". Yes, definitely, LOVE is stronger than DEATH. Pat does dwell in me and I in her forever.

May 21, 2017
Pat says make FB posts more helpful to others

Grief is a tough journey but Pat is with me. She has switched to a journal for writing messages to me - no more scrolling by too fast for me to read. Now a wallpaper sized sheet of paper that is very clear and I can easily move about on and read. It is in her own hand.

Recent message. "Your posts are too much about our destiny; make them more useful to those that need help on their grief journey." There are lots of love poems on it but I'd have to memorize them to make copies. I'm only in that between wake and sleep stage not enough time to see the journal - 5 minutes at most - not enough time. It is enough that they are for me. Thank you, Love! Pat, I love you forever!

May 22, 2017
Lilacs

A spouse's death leaves an emptiness that is hard to fill and you don't really want to fill - it is her place in you! There's no one in the house with whom to share the events of the day, discuss the dusty steps and rotten politics. Aside from the pain of personal loss, I feel intense pain for what she lost, especially the blossoming of our two granddaughters and of course, this time of year, the blooming of her favourite lilacs. Pat, I love you forever.
Well I did it on May 19th. The first lilacs from our backyard are now on Pat's grave. Hope after I'm no longer able someone in the family will take over bringing lilacs to our grave every spring. If there are lilacs in Heaven I'll bet that Pat knows where they are!

May 25, 2017
We are born again!

What if the earth is a womb, the soul an embryo and death
a birth into eternity? Could it be this is what Christ meant
in John 3:3 (KJV) "Jesus answered and said unto him,
Verily, verily, I say unto thee, except a man be born
again, he cannot see the kingdom of God?" Our life on
earth is our soul being formed in the womb of mother
earth and searching for our soulmate to make us whole in
the image of God in Heaven. It could also explain why
Christ had to die – the cross was His final step in His
preparation for assuming his resurrection body, man being
reborn into eternity and of course His victory over Death.
Pat was my true love who united with me in the
spirituality of sacrifice and oblation that is marriage. Ours
was a sacramentally and mystically union. We became
true soulmates, our souls directed together by God. We
were no longer two but one as God intended. Our love
grew – as Pat said "…our marriage … I thought was
getting better & better, and visualized it getting better
indefinitely for the rest of our lives. I think the stronger
you grow in yourself, the more you can love another
person." By the twenty year of our marriage we suffered
separation trauma when either one was away from the
other over night. We had moved into the final trimester of
our development for resurrection "and in the dead season /
the death of the leaves. / foretells a new dawn / near our

167

thresholds. / Incense rolls towards / the skies from the secrets / of the altars." – (Untitled poem fragment by Patricia A. Bow 1983?)

Over the years our love grew stronger and stronger and we two grew more alike. It helped that we started out very alike. She started out as a better person than I as well as a happier person. I think I grew both in caring and happiness. But Pat wasn't always pleased especially when she saw some of my mother creeping around in me. In middle age Pat seemed to pick up my melancholia and self doubt. I'm sorry I had that effect on the beautiful person she was. Pat passed away Saturday, January 7, 2017 at 5 pm. Now I feel she has peace even as she sometimes shows frustration with me.

The loss of a spouse makes you feel entirely alone and incomplete. The sense of feeling like you have lost an essential part of yourself is both painful and disconcerting. But I believe in the sacrament of marriage where God joins two entities into one and that although, death separates the physical entities, the spiritual entity made by God remains united; half in my heart the other half in heaven. I believe this with all my being; I really haven't lost Patricia I have gained Christ; I am one with her in the arms of Christ in Heaven and she is still one with me in my heart. Now that should bring closure and great joy, right? So, why am I still grieving? I want her touch, kisses and words now more than ever. The tears are mostly for the loss of these. I rejoice in her PEACE and in the prospect of once again being fully one with her in Heaven.

I believe that neither death, nor life, nor angels, nor principalities, nor powers, nor things present, nor things to come, nor height, nor depth, nor any other thing, shall be able to separate us (that is Pat and I) from the love of God and from each other united in Holy Matrimony. And I believe in the resurrection of the body, and the life of the world to come, through our Lord Jesus Christ; who shall change our mortal bodies into a resurrection body, that be like unto His glorious body.

Yes, I believe that Pat and I are not even separated by the death of Pat, since her spirit continues to live with me not yet deceased. And this continues until my death, when we meet again and reunite and loving each other more tenderly than before because we are in eternity. I believe that Pat really does dwell within me and I dwell within her. Her presence is getting stronger every day! Love is stronger than death. I also believe our love is continuing to grow ever stronger.

Every time I am depressed and feeling low, Pat comforts me. She shows me her poems or what poems she was reading, she sends me a pleasant dream, she types a message on that screen I sometimes see in the haze of waking up, she kisses or touches me... How can I doubt she dwells within me and I dwell within her? We will dwell in our place in heaven for ever more. My cup over flows. She is for me the good shepherd's servant.

I do not have to come all the way to Pat in Heaven, because she is also coming to me. I already have that empty hole in me to let her in. We are still two individuals united into one trinity by marriage and love. Our love is still growing stronger as is her presence in me. Pat is not here physically and that does make me feel lonely but, our most precious memories are still within me and it is easier now to call them up at well. Pat, I love you forever.

May 26, 2017 at 12 noon
Dwelling she in me and I in her

This morning as I awoke I saw in that waking haze, a bright light above me and just toward the right where the windows are but, a lot stronger then the dawn light. I left my body, to rise up to become that light. I was looking down at myself lying in the bed. Then I was at the Royal Botanical Garden's Lilac Dell and seeing the lilacs right up close and smelling them. It then occurred to me I was looking through Pat's eyes - that I was in her. I felt her peace and comfort.

Then after a brief nap while waiting for a laundry to finish for the drier, in the waking haze images of Pat – a slide show of her, each picture prettier than the last, all a perfect, gorgeous, healthy glowing Pat. At the end, the usual journal with love poems scrolled by – stopping at one line in her own hand "I love you, you and only you." And then the lines from her 12th Anniversary Poem,

underlined for emphasis; "yet beneath the grass and stone / intertwined their roots have grown, / so intimately webbed together, / neither one can tell his own."
Now these two "dreams" where a beautiful, mystical experience. Just thinking of them brings tears of JOY to my eyes. Surely goodness and loving kindness will follow me all the days of my life, and I shall dwell in Pat and she shall dwell in me and we shall dwell in the house of the LORD forever.

June

Philippians 1:21-23 (KJV)

21 For to me to live is Christ, and to die is gain.

22 But if I live in the flesh, this is the fruit of my labour: yet what I shall choose I wot not.

23 For I am in a strait betwixt two, having a desire to depart, and to be with Christ; which is far better:

June 1, 2017
Pat's morning message to me

Often as I wake in the mornings I see the journal Pat is
keeping in Heaven. "Is it real, or is it hallucination?" is
not the issue; it makes no difference. For me the journal is
real -- answering my questions comforting me and
enriching my life.

Today, Pat's morning message to me written in her
journal:

There is no being called; God does NOT take us; He
accepts us. Give up this idea that there is NO place for
you in Heaven. I am here and preparing our place in
Heaven.
"You love me royally, as I love you,
seated together in our garden Kingdom,
keeping up our silent conversation,
clothed in robes of joy of every hue."

Yes, our love was unique and rare. God see all. He sees
how the three of us – you, me, and our quiet love –
became the one triune entity we were meant to be. Garden
Kingdom, Garden of Eden, Heaven, all three are one; we
were headed there from the first.
"For us, our royal love has had no parallel:
It rooted, grew, and like a miracle

spread to the garden where in now we sit,
Clothed in the fragrance of fulfillment."

We are still on that journey to discover the inner self in
each other. No there is no one who knows me or you
better than ourselves and each other. Please stop fretting.
All those "silent conversations," our quiet love and our
always being together saw to that.
"And this long miracle is to discover
the inmost me and you,
to nurse no longing for another,
to forge the soul and its desire together
gently, openly and forever."

We will be reunited into the one that our marriage made
us; marriage in heaven is a unity of souls in the image of
the Divine Trinity. It is Christ Himself not the Bible, who
is the true Word of God. And after all He is in Heaven
and married – to the Church. So, there is marriage in
Heaven.
"Nothing grows but common flowers
outside our Kingdom's wall.
Here alone the magic lies.
We ask nothing; we have all."

Well this was very comforting. Adapting Pat's 1974
words: I think I could live contentedly through any crisis
that might come, as long as I know I can depend on Pat's

presence in me. Pat was and is the only woman for me, and without her I would be all disorganized fragments of grief. Love is stronger than Death. Pat, I love you forever.

Monday June 5, 2017
Kingdom of Heaven is within

"A lot of Christians ... assume that the Kingdom of Heaven means the place where you go when you die -- if you've been good. But the problem with this interpretation is that Jesus himself specifically contradicts it when he says, "The Kingdom of Heaven is within you" (that is, here) and "at hand" (that is, now). It's not later, but lighter -- some more subtle quality or dimension of experience accessible to you right in the moment. You don't die into it: you awaken into it" -- Cynthia Bourgeault in 'The Wisdom of Jesus".

This has tremendous implications.

For me this hit home almost immediately on my Grief Journey. The Kingdom of Heaven is here, now and within me! Combine this with Christ's words on the cross in Luke 23:43 and Paul's in I Corinthians 5:6-8, Philippians 1:23, and I Thessalonians 4:15-16 which tell us that when we die our soul is immediately with Christ in Heaven. It means your beloved spouse upon death goes immediately to heaven which is within us here and now and we feel her through Christ within us now and forever.

When Pat visited and kissed me the day after she died, it was REAL! She was already with Christ and within me; so, appearing to me and kissing me was an out of body experience for both of us. It was also a confirmation that the sacrament of marriage had united us as one entity forever.

You would think that grasping all this would take away the sorrow and the grief. Obviously, it didn't. The depression and sorrow keeps periodically returning and I so miss her physical presence. WHY, when Christ promises she is with me though himself?

My niece had a 'truth most true answer'; she wrote: "Because it does - you don't exist exclusively on a spiritual plane (yet). This is the rest of you (physical, emotional) processing the loss of her physical and emotional presence on a daily basis. Perfectly normal for this to roll over you and for you to feel those losses in a day to day existence."

"You don't die into it: you awaken into it," also hit home. For me it means you grow into heaven by meditation and searching within yourself. For me the proof of this is my feeling closest to Pat and Christ when I meditate during the mass. I appreciate a priest who allows long periods of silence during the service for meditation and thinking on your loved ones. Jesus is calling us to awake and hear him speaking from within "Who hath ears to hear, let him hear" (Mathew 13:9 KJV) Christ is the true word of God and He is within you now.

You don't have to wait to see your departed loved one because Heaven is within you and she is also (in the arms of Christ) within you. You do have to listen to that voice within and use your mind's eye. "… blessed are your eyes, for they see: and your ears, for they hear" Matthew 13:16 KJV.

Serene light shining in the ground of my being,
Draw me to yourself.
Draw me past the snares of the senses,
Out of the mazes of the mind,
Free me from symbols, from words
That I may discover the signified:
The word unspoken in the darkness
That veils the ground of my being.
  -Byzantine Hymn

Friday June 20, 2017
Essential truths

My five essential truths that are most true:
1. Love is from God, and whoever loves has been born of God and knows God.
2. Love is stronger than death even though it can't stop death from happening, but no matter how hard death tries it can't separate people from love.
3. I love Pat and Pat loves me forever.

4. By marriage two are united into one, a Trinity in the image of God.

5. Pat dwells in me and I dwell in her through God for all eternity.

Sunday June 11, 2017
Born a Scot....

In the past 48 years, there is no moment or event I took pleasure in or enjoyed where Patricia Bow was not present. We were that much together: we really were one person. We wouldn't have had it any other way. Even now when I think of going somewhere or doing something I'm thinking of Pat and I doing or going to it together. It just wouldn't be the same without Pat there with me. I realize it is the thought that if she had lived in six days we would have been boarding VIA's Atlantic for a repeat (with train being a pleasant addition) of our 2003 Nova Scotia anniversary celebration that is making me sad right now. Pat had another dream of us being hermits by the ocean; but note again she was thinking of us being one entity. When I was growing up I wanted and wished I had been born a Scot. Well in marring Pat and becoming one with her I guess I did become a Scot. I think the one we became would eventually have planned a trip to see the Cameron Clan home. Looking at pictures of Ben Nevis, Loch Linnhe, and Fort William I am sure we would have enjoyed it as much as Nova Scotia. I can feel Pat within me approving. Now that is not to say I'll be doing such a trip. I'm content living with Pat dwelling in me and I in her.

Monday June 11, 2017
Pat and I united as one

Pat also enjoyed our togetherness and being one. At parties, even with family you would find her either next to me or making frequent contact across a crowded room. When she went out with her sisters, "girl's time out". she enjoyed it but the enjoyment wasn't complete until she told me all about it and went to the new place with me after in the days following. Thanks to her oldest sister we discovered some great tea houses around KW. Pat and I were soul mates wanting what was best for each other. Oh, she occasionally needed a walk about alone with her thoughts and to sit and prey alone with God but all writers need this. Now we both are content dwelling within each other through God. I think we are nearly there to C. S. Lewis' "God and us" - Christ certainly is first in our triune unity.

Tuesday June 13, 2017
You don't have a soul. You are a Soul. You have a body

I have experienced after-death contacts with Pat while awake or dreaming, via the usual senses. I can almost call these up by prayer and meditation. I become quiet and peaceful in both and that seems to bring Pat right there when I cry her name.

It has occurred to me as Pat's presence within me grows ever stronger, I will lose seeing her with my physical senses. (Sheldon Vanauken's second death or severe mercy.) Souls do not use the physical senses or even words to communicate with each other. Our soul is who we are; it is the entity that unites with another in marriage and with the God within us. "You don't have a soul. You are a Soul. You have a body." In other words, personhood is not based on having a body. A soul is what is required. It is eternal. The soul communicates on the ethereal/spiritual/astral level - feeling not speaking.

In marriage, the one entity created by God in the sacrament of marriage is also a soul for all eternity. In the Garden of Eden, there were three present, and there was joy. So, if God is central in a marriage today, there also will be joy. Without God, a true and full oneness is not possible. Pat's 1970 anniversary poem says it all:

You love me royally, as I love you,
seated together in our garden Kingdom,
keeping up our silent conversation,
clothed in robes of joy of every hue.
For us, our royal love has had no parallel:

It rooted, grew, and like a miracle
spread to the garden where in now we sit,
Clothed in the fragrance of God in it.

And this long miracle is to discover
the inmost me and you,
to nurse no longing for another,
to forge the soul and its desire together
gently, openly and forever.

Nothing grows but common flowers
outside our Kingdom's wall.
Here alone the magic lies.
We ask nothing; we have all.

I find I feel Pat within me most when I am praying,
meditating and during the sacrament. 1 Corinthians 10:16
The cup of blessing which we bless, is it not the
communion of the blood of Christ? The bread which we
break, is it not the communion of the body of Christ?
King James Version (KJV). I find Pat there with Christ
and among the communion of saints. I know as her
presence in me grows stronger I'm going to depend more
on Christ and this communion of souls for her presence
and for communication with her (also, on my dreams).
Faith in Christ is a gift of God, and we can believe the
gospel only when God gives us a new heart that is open to
the preaching of His Word (John 3:5; Eph. 2:8). Christ

himself is the only true Word of God and He is in our Heart. Of course, everyone who has been given such a heart and presence will finally trust in the wisdom of Christ alone for salvation and that our loved one dwells in us. Now THAT is C. S. Lewis' meaning of a marriage coming to "God and us.

Thursday Jun 15, 2017

Behold, the kingdom of God is within you

I believe a person who has Faith in the Lord Jesus Christ as his Savior goes immediately to heaven to be in the presence of the Lord when he dies. Though their body is in the grave and either ashes or decomposing, their soul and spirit (the immaterial part, the real person) goes immediately into the presence of God. - it is the measurable slight weight loss at death. Christ did and he was both man and God. Scripture said as much, it reports in Luke 23:43 that He said to the thief on the cross next to Him "And Jesus said unto him, Verily I say unto thee, today shalt thou be with me in paradise."

And Paul says in Phil. 1:21-23. "For to me, to live is Christ, and to die is gain. 22 But if I am to live on in the flesh, this will mean fruitful labor for me; and I do not know which to choose. 23 But I am hard-pressed from both directions, having the desire to depart and be with Christ, for that is very much better;"

I admit to also having the desire to be with Christ (and Pat) and live in Christ. But according to Luke 17:21 (KJV) "Neither shall they say, lo here! or, lo there! for, behold, the kingdom of God is within you." You don't have to die to join your departed spouse - she is in the kingdom of God within you here and now. Pat dwells in me and I dwell in her here and now.

I realize some Christians may call this heresy and cite other texts that support their view. My texts are also in the Bible. Then there is this, a favorite from Cynthia Bourgeault in 'The Wisdom Jesus': "A lot of Christians … assume that the Kingdom of Heaven means the place where you go when you die — if you've been good. But the problem with this interpretation is that Jesus himself specifically contradicts it when he says, "The Kingdom of Heaven is within you" (that is, here) and "at hand" (that is, now). It's not later, but lighter — some more subtle quality or dimension of experience accessible to you right in the moment. You don't die into it: you awaken into it" You reach it by searching within yourself."

I have experienced my wife's presence within me and I assure you she is NOT sleeping in wait for some future Judgement Day. She is very much awake and communing with me. Nor are the Communion of Saints, whose fellowship we rejoice in during Communion, asleep - they are very much awake giving us that fellowship we pray for during the Communion service. "It is Christ Himself," *Lewis* said, "*not the Bible*, who is the true *word of God*." So, listen to what your soul is telling you. Don't use Scripture as a weapon.

Thursday June 15, 2017
 Still crying…

I came home from a nice lunch with my friend and started to put away some winter scarves and hats Pat had knitted

185

for herself and me. As I was folding them I was over come by extreme grief. I started to cry like a baby. I was noisy, shaken and crying hard. Still feel a bit weepy. I miss her so much. My physical being is crying for her physical touch and kisses. Pat, I love you forever.

Friday June 16, 2017
Feeling like old Adam…

Yes, my grief makes me:
"feel like old Adam at the end of that sixth day, /
just a boy rubbing his fingers over the fresh/
stitches in his side, wondering why me? why here?"/
 (apologies to John Blase).

Last night (June 15/16) she was happy, wrote in her journal, "Turning 71 on my birthday, but, I am happy because my beloved Eric joins me." It was almost too much to bear because I want so much to be there in heaven with her. The Kingdom of Heaven is within and she lives within me, this keeps me sanely grounded. I believe she meant "We will see what a bright heaven is around us. We are one growing ever stronger in our love and in each other. We will forever feel heaven's joys in each other more ravishingly shared in the company of each other. And of course I join her every day – I awake unto her soul within me every morning. On her birthday, there will be a revelation bringing us even closer together. The Kingdom of God is here and now and I'm already in it through her. But if she meant more - she knows when I will come fully home - so be it. God's will be done on earth as it is in Heaven.

Pat will welcome me up into heaven when my time comes, to meet her there, and to continue to dwell within her there, when my death has come: three persons - her, me and our love forever united as one - a trinity of love - LOVE is stronger than Death - I will receive from her royal welcome, warmer and more joyous than ever was given, in the outburst of conjugal affection, to any returning from an absence upon earth. I will hear her loving voice again and see her again amid the light of a glorious eternity. We will be at home in our place in Heaven promised by Christ.

Sunday June 18, 2017
Communion during Grief....

Today after the 8 am Mass I met with a gentleman who had just lost his wife of 68 years. Fr. Victor introduced him to me - we were the last three in the Church. Poor man was still in the very early stages of his Grief Journey. He was sobbing. I exchanged some of what I had experienced during my journey and some of the truths my journey has brought to me. It seemed to help. We both agreed the Mass was and is a big help. Our tears gave each of us permission to cry. I am glad that I was able to help. It is good to cry together, pray together and take communion together. Our Faith keeps us grounded and sane. God gives us grace to rejoice in the fellowship of all who have gone before us and to be with and through them partakers of His heavenly kingdom. We are united with our departed spouses forever.

Monday June 19, 2017
Memory merge...

Just a thought: Could it be, as your departed loved one's presence in you grows ever stronger, your memories strengthen each other's and thus become more vivid and true? You see the event with both your eyes and feel it with both your hearts. Case in point, I remember us in the Blackshop Restaurant on her 70th birthday but, now see the table surroundings from both our eyes as a complete surround view. As I write this the feeling grows stronger and the surround view clearer. Interesting.

Tuesday June 20, 2017
A Comforting thought

Part of Grief is your mind refusing to accept the death of your loved one and wishing it had not happened. That is why the tears come at witnessing another couple of your age doing the everyday loving things you used to do - holding hands on a walk, stealing a secret kiss on the street, etc. The mind won't accept she is actually gone and the spied-on couple remind you of happier times. The Grief only lessens when your mind accepts she is dead and her soul is both with Christ and within you. That emptiness and pain you feel around your heart, it is her. Accepting her presence within you is the key - rejoice in it and receive comfort from it. Feel what she is feeling - the Peace which passes all understanding - in Christ's arms. LOVE is stronger than DEATH! Celebrate He who is LOVE and won the victory over death. Only then are you able to say, "O death, where is thy sting? O grave, where is thy victory?"

Wednesday June 21, 2017
48th anniversary.

If the presence of Pat I feel and sometimes see were self-hypnosis or figments of my imagination then on days like today - our 48th anniversary - I surely would see more of them because it is my mind's desperate wish to see and feel them. Today was a hard day with no special presence of Pat. Oh she was there as always in my heart but that is usual and not the something special like the kiss the day after she died. There was no quality presence - a presence you just know is her soul, her very essence, her person, her intelligence and her love. Yes, she lives both in me and in the arms of Christ.

Thursday June 22, 2017
Memories

When Pat was happiest after our marriage it was always
just her and me. She would ritualise her happy moments.
The PBS series "Jewel in the Crown was among the first.
She'd get herself comfortable. Curl up in a chair with her
favourite treats and her cuppa tea around her and one of
her craft projects, me close by and watch with pleasure.
Neither of us needed company to enjoy life – we had each
other and our rituals. Christmas Eve was a ritual that that
included her sisters – we'd exchange places with her sister
Deanna (one year Dani's place the next year ours (so glad
Deanna and Bette came over Christmas Eve 2016) and
always ending with Pat and I going to the late Mass.
Sundays were always special. After Church we'd come
home, make lunch (I'd buy Zehr's wings and wedges, Pat
would make a freshly made grilled cheese - - had to be
real aged cheddar) and we'd listen to the Vinyl Café. The
last show was Dec 23, 2016 and Stuart Mclean died just a
few weeks after Pat. Her life and her favourite moments –
events we had ritualized all seemed to end at the same
time. Life without Pat and these rituals of happiness is
hard to bear but the memories are so pleasant and still
bring a warmth to my heart. Memories of us at the Oban
Inn, in Stratford listening to BargeMusic, the Grand
Philharmonic Choir performing Handel's Messiah at the
start of the Christmas season, etc. I have so many

memories of us being happy together. Thank you, my beloved, for a great marriage and life together. So, looking forward to spending all eternity together in the arms of Christ. Love is stronger than Death.

Saturday June 24, 2017
God and us

Pat and I were soulmates. Soulmate relationships are far and few but when they do occur, they are for eternity. This kind of relationship is marked by an intense connection between two people, two souls, one that may even be difficult to convey in words. Two people just "get each other" — they finish each other's sentences, are best friends, and have adopted the us against the world mentality, and a us and God outlook. It feels like we are two pieces of a puzzle fitting perfectly together. In the six months from our first date to our marriage we found each other's souls and bonded. The sacrament of marriage bound our two souls into a Trinity - one entity, three persons. I still feel that haunting familiarity. There is a knowing we are at home in each other's hearts. We both look forward to coming home to each other in heaven. Pat on our 48th anniversary did write in her heavenly journal I am allowed to read through her eyes, "I'll be 71 on my next birthday but I am happy because my beloved Eric joins me." I'll be ready. 'God and us' is very close and possible.

Te lucis ante terminum.

BEFORE the ending of the day,
Creator of the world, we pray
That with thy wonted favour thou
Wouldst be our guard and keeper now.

From all ill dreams defend our eyes,
From nightly fears and fantasies;
Tread under foot our ghostly foe,
That no pollution we may know.

O Father, that we ask be done,
Through Jesus Christ, thine only Son;
Who, with the Holy Ghost and thee,
Doth live and reign eternally. Amen.

THE BOOK OF COMMON PRAYER

www.ingramcontent.com/pod-product-compliance
Lightning Source LLC
LaVergne TN
LVHW011349080426
835511LV00005B/208